SIR WALTER: A FOUR-PART STUDY IN BIOGRAPHY

WALTER SCOTT
From a picture by H. Raeburn

[*Frontispiece*

SIR WALTER: A FOUR-PART STUDY IN BIOGRAPHY

(SCOTT, HOGG, LOCKHART, JOANNA BAILLIE)

BY

DONALD CARSWELL

HASKELL HOUSE PUBLISHERS LTD.

Publishers of Scarce Scholarly Books

NEW YORK. N. Y. 10012

1971

First Published 1930

HASKELL HOUSE PUBLISHERS LTD.
Publishers of Scarce Scholarly Books
280 LAFAYETTE STREET
NEW YORK. N. Y. 10012

Library of Congress Catalog Card Number: 70-176490

Standard Book Number 8383-1365-5

Printed in the United States of America

PREFACE

I BEGAN this book with the intention of writing a short study of Scott, to be followed by sketches of perhaps half a dozen of his many distinguished friends. But before I had gone very far I had to succumb to the fascination of the principal figure and change my plan. For the life of Scott is the strangest drama in literary biography, and the strangest thing about it is that never was a man of genius so ordinarily and appealingly human, alike in his strength and his frailty, his simplicity and his tortuousness, the greatness of which he was barely conscious, and the littleness that meant all the world to him.

All these things are commonplace to any informed and critical reader of Lockhart's classic *Life*, but the ordinary reader is apt to miss them, as they are by no means explicit. In spite of his brilliant handling of his material, Lockhart was handicapped nearly as much as he was helped by the special relation in which he stood to his subject, with the result that his portrait, vivid and truthful as it is, is severely abstract. The Scott it depicts is the Scott of the study, the domestic circle and polite society. We get no clear view of Scott, the man of the world and business. Of Scott's business affairs, indeed, Lockhart knew little more than that the subject was a disagreeable one which he had neither the will nor the capacity to understand. Yet the course of Scott's business dealings constitutes the whole tragedy of Abbotsford—for a tragedy it was rather than the epic that Lockhart chose to make of it, and which incidentally caused him to be grossly unfair to Scott's fellow-sufferers, Archibald Constable and James Ballantyne.

It is in this tragic perspective that I have tried to reconstruct the outlines of Scott's life. The essential story is told in the first half of the book. The second half is devoted to three intimate friends whose lives serve to reflect aspects of Scott without which the picture would be incomplete, but which for the sake of clearness had to be disregarded in the main narrative.

I am indebted to Lieut.-Col. John Murray, Mr. John Buchan and my wife, Catherine Carswell, for much valuable help and criticism; and I have to thank my friend Dr. Isabel Emslie Hutton for a hitherto unknown letter of Scott, and the Rev. H. T. Carnegie, Vicar of Hampstead, for permission to reproduce the portrait of Joanna Baillie that is preserved in the vestry of Hampstead Parish Church.

D. C.

HAMPSTEAD,
February 11th, 1930.

CONTENTS

LIST OF ILLUSTRATIONS

SIR WALTER SCOTT

THERE are few contrasts in history more remarkable than that which prevailed between North and South Britain in the eighteenth century. For England the character of the eighteenth century consisted, not in its events, important as these were, but in its culture. It was not so much an epoch as a philosophy. Its guiding principle, equilibrium, was applied rigorously to every department of life (except perhaps the convivial) and with conspicuous success to the business of government. Englishmen felt secure ; and if their security engendered self-satisfaction, it did at least allow them to cultivate their gardens to some purpose. Unfortunately, the philosophy of equilibrium was unable to cross the Tweed. For Scotland the eighteenth century had an entirely different meaning and content, which are reflected even in the romantic idealisations of the period that are current to-day. To the English mind the eighteenth century conjures up an agreeable picture of Beau Nash, Dr. Johnson, foxhunting squires, bottle-nosed parsons and hearty inn-keepers. To the Scot it is the century of Rob Roy and Prince Charlie—an unstable, adventurous, even heroic century, full of bitter-sweet memories. It was in fact an era that, so far from being static, was marked by violent and bewildering change.

This was but natural. Change had been long overdue. From the fatal day of Flodden to the Treaty of Union the history of Scotland exhibits nothing that can be reasonably regarded as progress—nothing, that is, analogous to the definite cultural phases which the sixteenth and seventeenth centuries represent in the history of England. There was the Reformation, of course, and it would be absurd to discount its effect on the national character and the course of history. But it is equally absurd to ascribe to it a cultural value that it certainly did not possess. For the Scottish Reformation was not tempered, as in England and on the Continent, by the Renaissance. The Scottish aristocracy who exploited it for their own ends had no use for the New Learning or learning of any kind. They vented their hatred and contempt of all such notions on the defenceless body of Rizzio ; and even John Knox, who could record the " Knave Davie's " bloody end with sour satisfaction, found himself doubting the integrity of his noble allies when they mutilated his scheme of national education. In the seventeenth century the Kirk's only achievement was to involve Scotland in the Civil War on terms that said more for its zeal than its intelligence. For two hundred years, in fact, Scotsmen were eager to do anything but set their own house in order. Their polity—tribalism in the North and a disparate feudalism in the South—remained anomalous and antiquated, and when the seventeenth century closed they were still in all essentials a mediæval people, with this difference from their condition in the actual Middle Ages, that they had impoverished their country, destroyed their churches and, by ceasing to cultivate literature, had even lost their language.

The change with which the eighteenth century opened was a drastic one. It was called a Parliamentary Union, but in effect it was the merger of the Scottish Parliament and Executive in the Parliament and Executive of England. But even so it was only a half-measure. A feeble Parliament and a corrupt Privy Council had gone, but the ancient heritable jurisdictions, which constituted the real power in Scotland, remained intact. Twice during the next forty years the country was convulsed by civil war, and after Charles Edward's Rebellion, it was clear that stability and progress were impossible so long as the chiefs and barons retained their privileges. The heritable jurisdictions were accordingly abolished, and Scotsmen began the task of aligning themselves with the century in which they lived. The era of the agricultural " improvers " set in and changed the whole aspect of the Scottish countryside. Commerce and industry expanded. Literature was again cultivated—English literature, it is true, yet with a distinct flavour of peat-reek that gave it character. These innovations, of course, were not made without opposition. In particular the efforts of men like William Robertson and Alexander Carlyle to imbue the Kirk with the spirit of the age were only a qualified success ; for they provoked the reactionary manifestations which started Scottish Presbyterianism on its long and discreditable career of schism.

The social and economic reconstruction of Scotland was accomplished within the compass of three score and ten years, so that a man born at the beginning of the century might well live to see the mediæval country of his childhood assuming the first drab tints of industrialism. Such a one was Robert Scott, farmer and stockbreeder, of Sandyknowe, Roxburghshire, who died in 1775, and he was typical of his changeful day, being the first member of his family that ever turned his hand to honest work. For his blood was reckoned " gentle "—that is to say, his ancestors had lived by cattle-stealing and other adventures suitable to their dignity. As the cattle-stealing industry declined during the latter part of the seventeenth century, many old Border families (especially the cadet branches) were sorely pinched. Robert Scott's father, for example, had to live in genteel poverty on the pittances he received by purporting to manage estates for certain relatives. He was a fantastical old Tory, who gained the nickname of " Beardie " because he took and kept a vow never to shave or trim his beard while the Stuarts remained in exile. This descendant of Border " reivers " was also a great pedant, exceeding proud of his Latinity, and a crony of Dr. Archibald Pitcairn.

Robert Scott had nothing in common with his father except his furious obstinacy. They quarrelled. Robert went his own way, proclaimed himself a Whig, took to farming and, being an unrivalled judge of livestock, did very well for himself. He had a large family. His eldest son, Walter, he bred to the law, which was yet another new departure in the Scott family and indicates Farmer Robert's shrewdness. For Walter was not the kind of lad to make a successful farmer. There was a dash of old " Beardie " in him, which was bound to handicap him in any walk of life and in farming would be fatal. Besides, as Robert Scott noted, the legal profession in Scotland was entering a period of prosperity and consequence such as it had never known before. *Cedant arma togæ.* The arbitrament of the sword had gone out of fashion, but the nobility and gentry were as pugnacious as ever and now fought their battles in the Court of Session. There was an undoubted future in the law in those days.

Accordingly Walter Scott was sent to Edinburgh to be apprenticed to a Writer to the Signet.

He began his indentures in time to see the Young Chevalier ride in triumph up the High Street, and all his life he had cause to keep the "Forty-five" in mind. As a good Whig he would deplore it, but as an attorney he could look back upon it with equanimity. It brought clients; for the forfeitures and other sequelæ of the Rebellion yielded a considerable volume of legal business of a kind well suited to a man of Mr Scott's laborious and economical disposition. For the rest, his clients were mainly litigious lairds and farmers of the Border counties. In 1758, when he had been some years in practice, he married Anne Rutherford, whose father was professor of botany at the University—an eminently suitable alliance for a young professional man. He prospered and brought up a family.

Mr. WALTER SCOTT, W.S., had excellent qualities. He was diligent and scrupulous, and he knew a great deal of law. He was a man of spotless reputation, sincerely religious and as devoted to the Presbyterian order as " Beardie " had been to Prelacy. He overflowed with admirable intentions, though these were not always appreciated by his clients. Mild and even melancholy in temper, he could, it has been alleged, be almost gay over a moderate glass of wine when the obligations of hospitality absolutely demanded it; he played his regular round of golf; and his Calvinism, strict as it was, did not foreclose him from performing on the 'cello at the " gentlemen's concerts " in the Canongate or occasionally visiting the theatre that, in defiance of the godly, had been erected in the New Town. But apart from his dry-as-dust Latinity, of which he was as vain as old " Beardie," and his professional learning, which was certainly abstruse and curious, he had none of the attributes of an educated man. For him the Scriptures, the Westminster Confession, the Pandects, Stair's Decisions and Dirleton's Doubts made up the sum of wisdom, divine and human, outside of which all was vanity, and he viewed with sad-eyed perplexity a world that was somehow of another opinion. In his dealings he was apt to regard the eternal as well as the temporal interests of his clients, which anybody else would have realised was not good business. But business sense was never Mr. Scott's *forte*. He had a weakness for bad debts, for which he compounded by being rather stingy in his domestic arrangements. As he advanced in years his practice declined. A new generation found him what he in fact was—a tiresome, crotchety, pedantic, officious old man and also a good bit of a fool.

If Mr. Scott as a man of sixty could have been induced to give a candid opinion on the business of bringing up a family, he would probably have replied that, like most things, it partook largely of vanity and vexation of spirit. Anne Rutherford had, more or less cheerfully, borne him twelve children, of whom the first six died in infancy. The second six—five boys and a girl—were hardy enough to grow up, but they did not inspire their father with enthusiasm. They were certainly a plain-looking lot, though he could not complain of that : after all, he had not chosen Anne Rutherford for her looks, and the Scotts had never been beauties. Two of them were cripples—Annie through a long series of childish misadventures that had ended by leaving her a chronic invalid, and the third boy, Walter, who as a baby had had his right leg withered by poliomyelitis.

These were dispensations of Providence to be accepted without murmuring. What troubled Mr. Scott more was that none of his children showed any capacity or even inclination to minister to his pride. Robert, the eldest, was in the King's service (all honour to him), and he had some aptitude for music (which was more than any of the others had), but one liked him best when he was helping Admiral Rodney to fight the French. At home he was an evil-tempered bully. John, who was in the Army, was simply a dull dog. Annie—well, Annie's peculiarities might be excused for her many afflictions, and she was only a female. Tom was an amiable lad, but lacked gumption. Of Dan, the youngest, the less said the better.

On the whole Mr. Scott got most comfort from the contemplation of his third son and namesake, Walter, who was at the Bar, wherein was great cause for satisfaction and gratitude to the Power which directs even our afflictions to our good, for Wattie was of so venturesome and restless a disposition that he would assuredly have gone for a soldier had not Providence ordained him to hobble about on a stick all the days of his life. As it was, the lad had consented readily enough to be bound to the law, and, when his time was up, had pleased his father still more by electing to proceed to the Bar instead of sticking to a desk in George's Square. If Mr. Scott had known the motives of the choice he would have been less complacent about it. All he knew was that Walter had the best as well as the biggest head of the whole family, and there seemed to be no reason why, under proper guidance, he should not become the busiest man in Parliament House and end his days in the dignity of a Senator of the College of Justice. There was no doubt that he was a thoroughly competent lawyer. His father had seen to that. Years of merciless nagging had produced results that Mr. Scott could regard as on the whole satisfactory. Wattie's thesis for admission to the Faculty of Advocates (" Disputatio Juridica de Cadaveribus Punitorum," *Just. Dig.* lib. XLVIII, tit. xxiv) had been a very pretty piece of Latinity. On Mr. Scott's advice it had been dedicated to Lord Braxfield. There were things in his lordship's life and language that Mr. Scott deplored, but the scriptural advice to make friends with the mammon of unrighteousness may not lightly be disregarded, least of all when the mammon is Lord Justice-Clerk and, moreover, lives in the same square. Shortly after Walter's call a favourable opportunity of cultivating his lordship's acquaintance had occurred on circuit, but Walter, to his father's annoyance, had failed to seize it.

The fact that the young man had so far shown no forensic aptitudes whatever, being a poor orator and unready debater, caused Mr. Scott

no special concern. Practice would cure these
defects. Nor, solid Whig as he was, did he
complain of Wattie's Tory proclivities. As
politics stood, these favoured his professional
advancement, and in any case, what with
murdering, blaspheming Frenchmen abroad and
profligate traitors like Mr. Fox at home, it was
better for a young man in these days to be a
Jacobite than a Jacobin. But Mr. Scott could
not help wishing that Walter's walk and conversation showed more of the gravity of one
who has it in his heart to succeed in a grave
profession. He lived laborious days, it was
true ; but he did not scorn delights. In defiance
of the infirmity that Providence had laid upon
him, he was unreasonably addicted to violent
sports, despising golf. He was partial to light
men and light books. His boon-companion
was Willie Clerk, the ingenious Laird of Eldin's
younger son, but likewise a son of Belial.
" *Sicut aqua effusa est, non crescet,*" groaned Mr.
Scott at the mention of Willie Clerk's name.
" He goeth to dancing halls and readeth novels
—*sat est.*" In company with this and other
vain fellows Wattie had a deplorable habit of
strolling away into the country and forgetting to
return home for days together—" Nae better than
a gangrel scrapegut," as Mr. Scott said bitterly.

Not that there was any vice in Walter ; it was
just his misfortune that owing to his poor health
he had not been subjected to due discipline in

childhood. He had necessarily been indulged. He had spent far too much time at Kelso with his grandmother and aunt—worthy women, but foolish in the way of women with callants —who had not only exercised little supervision of his motions, but filled his head with godless tales and ballads of the Border, which it would have become them better as Christians to forget utterly. At home, too, his mother, who had liked to hear him read aloud, had not been sufficiently strict in the choice of literature, with the result that Wattie had got a taste for stage plays, novels, heroical poems and like trash that grieved his father very much indeed. It was an additional source of aggravation to Mr. Scott that he himself had not been blameless. Shortly after Walter had begun his apprenticeship, he had been sent on professional business into the Highlands. The client concerned was old Mr. Stewart, of Invernahayle, who was a worthy man, but had been " out " both in the Fifteen and in the Forty-five and was a little too fond of fighting his battles over again, especially when he could get a young and sympathetic listener. It had been a grave error of judgment sending Walter to Invernahayle. When he came home—bearing as trophies an old claymore and Lochaber axe presented by his appreciative host—his father had occasion to admonish him very seriously concerning " the blawing blazing stories which the Hieland gentlemen tell of those troublous times, which, if it were their will, they had better pretermit as tending rather to shame than to honour."[1] Altogether Walter was one of those whom the Apostle had in mind when he wrote: " Refuse profane and old wives' fables, and exercise thyself rather unto godliness : for bodily exercise profiteth little."

It was indeed vexing that even in one's own house and business one could not protect the manners of one's children from the corruption of evil communications. Thus, just about the same time as the Invernahayle episode, Thomas Grierson, one of Mr. Scott's own clerks, used to boast to Wattie of his intimacy with a lewd Ayrshire fellow of the baser sort that had come to Edinburgh and made a great stir among folk who ought to have known better. He had even suggested that Wattie should foregather with him and Mr. Burns at his lodgings, but, praise Heaven, nothing had come of it. By all accounts Mr. Burns was not a desirable acquaintance for any *impuber* or even *ephebus*. Wattie had had to be content with two distant glimpses of the poet—once in Professor Fergusson's drawing-room and once in Sibbald's circulating library, a place to which he was regrettably addicted. However, that was seven years ago—seven years during which Wattie had been systematically bullied and badgered,

[1] *Redgauntlet*, Letter IX

overworked and kept short of money. Mr. Scott could conscientiously say that he had left nothing undone for his son's welfare.

The subject of these loving solicitudes was a tall young man in the earliest twenties, whose big powerful frame and ruddy complexion showed no trace of the sickly, sallow child and youth that had been. His features were of the typical Scott cast—heavy, almost coarse— but he had a head such as never had been seen in the family, rising in a massive peak which later, when age had turned the light-brown hair to white, was singularly impressive. His countenance was serious but placid. His long upper lip had a whimsical twist, and when he smiled—which he did very engagingly—he showed a mouthful of strong beautiful teeth. His voice was deep and strong, and he spoke, not in the bleak and strident accents of Parliament House, but with a solid Border burr. In his manners he was, as young Scotsmen of his class and education usually are, juvenile and awkward ; but in the matter of dress, from being a notorious sloven, he had come to be reasonably neat. This reformation had been prompted by the onset of calf-love, the object of which was a very superior young lady, being (to old Mr. Scott's consternation) no less than the granddaughter of an earl. The affair, having gone on for several years in the most blameless romantic fashion, ended very happily in the marriage of the superior young lady to a superior young gentleman who was heir to a banking-house and a baronetcy. Walter's Parliament House cronies confidently expected an explosion, for the limping giant, though genial as a rule and the most diverting *raconteur* among the briefless who gathered round the fire in the Outer House, was very fierce and imperative when any fancy took his mind. But to the general amazement he was not even downcast. His first love-affair remained a precious memory, but he did not let it trouble his life. He kept it in storage. Keep a thing seven years, says the proverb, and you will find a use for it. It was twice seven years before Walter Scott found a use for the memory of Williamina Stuart (Lady Forbes, as she now was), but when found, it was a practical one. Meanwhile he consolidated his reputation as a *raconteur*, ate oysters in the Covenant Close, pursued curious literary studies, began to learn German (which had just come in as the latest romantic novelty) and did his honest best on the rare occasions when he found a set of papers in his box.

Scott's cool acceptance of his jilting is easily explained. He was not much in love with Miss Stuart of Fettercairn—at no time was he much of a lover of women—but he was very much in love with her noble birth, her elegant manners and the world in which she moved. For he had a spirited young man's full share of carking discontent with everything about him. He hated the careful dreary little world of professional Edinburgh to which his lameness and his father's austerity had condemned him. He did not like the Bar. The best that could be said was that it was better than being an attorney, which would have meant quarrelling with his father every day, and in any case was no profession " for a gentleman like me." He was a spirit in prison, and Miss Stuart had represented his dream of escape. Hitherto he had only had an imaginative release. He could wander in the unconfined past by declaiming a Border ballad or recalling one of old Invernahayle's blawing blazing stories. But that was not enough for Scott. Like many romantics, he was a thorough-paced materialist, and he demanded a material as well as a spiritual escape from his surroundings. In his eyes the nobility and gentry inhabited an earthly paradise in which he, as a Scott of Raeburn, might, with fortune, have a humble but undoubted place. Of this ambition the first really fine young lady he met would naturally become the symbol and incarnation. But since the rainy Sunday when he bashfully offered Miss Stuart a share of his umbrella as they came out of church, Walter Scott had matured by some years ; and about a year before she made her final decision, her effective place in his imagination had been usurped by a far more dazzling creature.

When the Court of Session rose in 1795, Scott went off to Kelso to spend the Long Vacation with his father's brother Robert. Presently he was writing to a friend a long letter full of chaste and artless speculations about his prospects with Miss Stuart, amid which he interpolated an exciting piece of news. " We have a great marriage towards here—Scott of Harden and a daughter of Count Brühl, the famous chess-player, a lady of sixteen quarters, half-sister to the Wyndhams. I wish they may come down soon, as we shall have fine racketing, of which I will, probably, get my share." They did come down soon and he did get his share of everything, including the favour of the new Lady of Harden—" the first woman of real fashion that took me up," as he said with complacent gratitude in later years. Harriet von Brühl had every possible claim upon Walter Scott's homage and admiration. She was the wife of his feudal chief and (he liked to think) distant kinsman. Her father was the Saxon Minister-plenipotentiary at St. James's. Her mother had been Countess of Egremont. Naturally, the granddaughter of a Scottish earl could not compare with this German lady of sixteen quarters and cosmopolitan culture. Walter Scott hastened to inform her that he adored the Germans and had some knowledge of their language. Harriet von Brühl may have wondered a little about the strange land she had come into, where young men of good standing talked such queer English and had no notion of aplomb in their conduct towards women. But this particular young savage had a promising look, and might repay attention. So she gave him her friendship, corrected his grammar, and taught him the elements of polite behaviour. She heard from him how difficult it was to get German books in Edinburgh, and how eager he was to get a sight of the late Gottfried Bürger's ballads, as he thought he could make a translation of *Lenore* that would be more spirited than any hitherto submitted to the British public. A copy of Bürger was soon forthcoming—Harriet sent to Hamburg for it —and Scott sat up all night, in wild excitement, making his translation, which so pleased him and his friends that he added a skull and cross-bones to the ornaments of his study and pro-ceeded to *Der Wilde Jäger*.

Those were great days for the high-flying romantics. Goethe and Schiller had at last joined forces. Bürger had died at the height of his reputation in 1794, and in the same year Mrs. Radcliffe had curdled the blood of young ladies to an ecstasy, exquisite but strictly chaste, with the *Mysteries of Udolpho*. Less exquisite and not at all chaste was a romance called *Ambrosio* or *The Monk*, which a very young, very undersized and very odd-looking gentleman in the Diplomatic Service, Lewis by name, had seen fit to throw upon the world in 1795. He got great fame by it. Robert Burns was dying at Dumfries, working even on his deathbed at his beloved task of preserving and restoring his country's folk-songs, and steadfastly refusing payment, though pinched for money. But Scott, absorbed in contemplation of his skull and crossbones, had lost interest in the national poet. As a lad he had been bitterly disappointed at the miscarriage of Tom Grierson's plan for a real meeting with Burns. As a young man, brimming over with literary enthusiasms and eager to make literary acquaintances, he could easily have repaired the omission. He knew Burns's friends the Riddels. Year after year, for months at a time, he was within an easy day's ride of Dumfries. Once, if not twice, in 1795 he was actually in the town. But he never sought out the poet, who would cheerfully have drunk with him till dawn. When Burns was dead, none was more earnest than Walter Scott in the empty business of his apotheosis. But Burns alive in Dumfries, broken in health and reputation, was a different proposition. Naturally, a socially ambitious young advocate would not seek the company of a crapulous Exciseman, with his shabby-genteel household, his peasant wife, his many bairns (not counting his bastards), who had disgraced himself among the local gentlefolk and was capable of advertising in shameless verse his amour with a blowsy barmaid at the Globe tavern. Scott's instinct was sound. A dubious contact was avoided. It is unlikely that he would have been happy with Burns. It is certain that Burns would have detested him. On July 25th, 1796, Burns's body was returned to its unkindly mother, with military honours rendered by the Dumfries Fencibles. Three months later Walter Scott's first published work issued from the press of Manners & Miller, Edinburgh. It was a thin quarto volume containing his two translations from Bürger. The German (and also the English) had been carefully checked by the kind Lady of Harden. Modesty, combining with professional prudence, kept him from putting his name on the title-page. The effort won the applause of his numerous young friends (who all had presentation copies), disgusted and distressed his poor father and left the public absolutely indifferent. Scott himself was well pleased. He was making little progress at the Bar, but it was something to have commenced author in the latest literary mode. His sense of importance was further gratified next spring when he was associated with the group of patriotic young gentlemen of condition who raised the Edinburgh Light Horse. Here was fate very handsomely defied. His lameness, though a hindrance, was not an absolute bar to service in a cavalry corps. He could now play at the fashionable game of soldiers with the best. He had no executive command, but as quartermaster, paymaster and secretary he cheerfully undertook all the regimental office-drudgery, for it was one of his conceits that, whatever might be said against his father's discipline, it had made a thorough business man of him. Poor old Mr. Scott! He had never dreamed of it being put to such a use. It was yet another instance of Wattie's reprobate delight in those things which are not convenient. What he would have thought of the crowning act of inconvenience that was to be committed in the autumn of 1797 we can only conjecture. A merciful stroke of apoplexy had intervened ere Walter announced his impending marriage to Charlotte Carpenter.

The sad old paralytic, straining his poor lips from time to time to frame some simple request of comfort or necessity, had no questions to ask. But other members of the family had. Who was this Miss Charlotte Carpenter? Walter's account was circumstantial on all but the material points. During the vacation, he and his soldier brother, John, and his friend, Adam Fergusson, had met her at the hotel at Gilsland Spa, near Penrith, in circumstances that left no doubt about her excellent social standing. She was the guest of the Dean of Carlisle and his wife, and was accompanied by a duenna who was the daughter of another dean and the granddaughter of a bishop. It was true that Miss Carpenter (*alias* Charpentier) was of French birth, but as she had been brought up in the Protestant faith, her principles of religion were very serious, and long residence in England, though it had not cured her accent, had so enlightened her understanding that she positively disapproved of the French. So far good, said Edinburgh, but who was she ? She was an orphan, and until she came of age had been the ward of the Marquess of Downshire. Her brother held high and lucrative office under the East India Company in Madras, and had covenanted to pay her an annuity of £500 or thereabouts, which would be very useful. That also was good to hear, but again came the fell Edinburgh query, who was the young person ? Walter had an answer,—" Well may I guess, but dare not tell," [1]—but it was never spoken. With what tact he could command he wrote to Charlotte asking for suitable information.

" You may tell your uncle," replied Charlotte peevishly, " that my brother is Commercial Resident at Salem. He will find the name of Charles C. in his India List. . . . I have no reason that can detain me in acquainting you that my father and mother were French, of the name of Charpentier ; he had a place under Government ; their residence was at Lyons, where you would find on inquiries that they lived in good repute and in *very good style*. I

[1] *The Wild Huntsman*, stanza 47.

had the misfortune of losing my father before I could know the value of such a parent. At his death we were left to the care of Lord Downshire, who was his very great friend, and very soon after I had the affliction of losing my mother. Our taking the name of Carpenter was on my brother's going to India, to prevent any difficulties that might have occurred. I hope now you are pleased."

Of course Scott was pleased. His relatives may have wished that the figure of the defunct Monsieur Charpentier of Lyons had been less shadowy, but they had to be content, and thenceforward the course of true love ran fairly smooth. Charlotte's noble guardian was more complacent than the Scott family, giving a gracious consent with only the most perfunctory inquiries on the subject of matrimonial finance. The statement of worldly prospects contained in Scott's letter of proposal would hardly have stood an audit, but it was accepted. That his income from the Bar was inconsiderable he freely granted, but what could Charlotte expect of one whose heart had lately been blighted and who, moreover, was an easy-going and unambitious young bachelor who could live in his father's house? There was no reason why he should not do well if he put his mind to it. Further, he was sanguine of legal preferment.

"I have every reason to expect that the Sheriffdom of a particular County, presently occupied by a gentleman in a very precarious state of health, may soon fall to my lot. The salary is £250 per annum and the duty does not interfere with the exercise of my profession, but greatly advances it. The only gentleman who can be entitled to dispute the situation with me is at present Colonel of a Regiment of Dragoons, an office which he will not readily quit for that of a provincial Judge. Many other little resources, which I cannot easily explain so as to make you comprehend me, induce me to express myself with confidence on the probability of my success."

To these assurances he added the earnest reassurance : " If you could form any idea of the society in Edinburgh, I am sure the prospect of living there would not terrify you." Charlotte was not so sure, but it was imperative that she should be decently settled in life. " I don't think that very thoughtful people ever can be happy," she wrote some weeks later. " As this is my maxim, adieu to all thoughts. I have made a determination of being pleased with everything and everybody in Edinburgh ; a wise system for happiness, is it not ? " So truly admirable a submission encouraged the bridegroom to enlarge upon the attractions of a Scottish marriage. His ancestors had been lords of broad lands, but had fallen on evil days.

" When you go to the south of Scotland with me, you will see their burying place, now all that remains with my father of a handsome property. It is one of the most beautiful and romantic scenes you ever saw, among the ruins of an old abbey. When I die, Charlotte, you must cause my bones to be laid there ; but we shall have many happy days before that, I hope."

Scott's bones, indeed! Edinburgh Charlotte was just prepared to accept. It was a hard fact that she had to face. But not Dryburgh. "If you always have these cheerful thoughts," she retorted, "how very pleasant and gay you must be!" Betrothal to a romantic and respectable young Scotsman might be a good thing, but it lacked *joie de vivre*. In the same letter—so serious was his love—he had actually asked if she would mind very much if he did not resign his commission in the Light Horse and sell his charger as a measure of economy. Charlotte protested with tact and spirit. "How very angry I should be if you were to part with Lenore! Do you really believe I should think it an *unnecessary expense* where your health and pleasure can be concerned? I have a better opinion of you, and I am very glad you don't give up the cavalry, as I love anything that is *stylish*."

On Christmas Eve, 1797, Walter Scott, advocate, had the honour of leading to the altar of St. Mary's Church, Carlisle, the natural daughter of Arthur, second Marquess of Downshire, by a Frenchwoman unknown.

There is a curious convention still observed in Scotland about the introduction of a bride to the bridegroom's friends. "An ill-favoured thing, sir, but mine own; a poor humour of mine, sir, to take that that no man else will: rich honesty dwells like a miser, sir, in a poor house, as your pearl in your foul oyster." In this unhandsome fashion poor Charlotte made her *début* in Edinburgh. "You may perhaps have remarked Miss C. at a Carlisle ball," wrote Scott to a friend three days before the wedding, " but more likely not, as her figure is not very *frappant*. A smart-looking little girl with dark-brown hair would probably be her portrait if drawn by an indifferent hand." Her moral qualities (in which nobody was interested and which were never notable) must be extolled, and her physical charms (which were undoubted) disparaged. The Ettrick Shepherd, who was a stranger to genteel conventions, got the impression that Mrs. Scott must be some kind of blackamoor. Actually, Charlotte was a very pretty, very lively, very French-looking brunette, and Scott, in spite of his Touchstone pose, admired her enormously. His simple vanity was flattered by the *furore* that her exotic appearance and manners created among his young friends. Her drawing-room in Castle Street became quite a *salon*, the regular resort of the Parliament House unemployed and the officers of the Edinburgh Light Horse. Scott was gratified to think that his wife was comparable, to some extent at least, with Scott of

Harden's—foreign birth, exalted lineage and all, though the latter, unfortunately, could only be hinted at. The older generation of Edinburgh folk were less favourably impressed. Charlotte was a daughter of Heth who sat in her drawing-room every day, and not on occasions of solemnity only, which was a sinful thing, seeing that only a generation earlier even the very best people in Edinburgh did not have drawing-rooms at all. But there was more substance than that in their censures. Charlotte had good looks and charm, and when the time came she played the outward part of Lady Scott of Abbotsford to perfection ; but she was shallow, ignorant, extravagant, pleasure-loving and thoroughly selfish. She did not love Scott. What passed for love was mainly a superstitious reverence for his power of making vast sums of money by means that were beyond her comprehension. Holding steadily by her silly cynicism about the incompatibility of thought with happiness, she lived a fairly happy life until, near the end, fate and her husband found her out.

But in those early days everything in the garden was lovely. The young couple had not much money—Charlotte's allowance from Madras proved to be more like £200 than £500, and it was a bumper year when Scott made two hundred guineas at the Bar—but they could afford a pleasant cottage at Lasswade in addition to the house in Castle Street. The hopes of legal preferment were brightening into certainty. Scott's enthusiastic volunteering had brought him to the notice of the Lord-Lieutenant of Midlothian, and the Lord-Lieutenant of Midlothian happened to be the Duke of Buccleuch, chief of the Scotts and territorial magnate whose interest was supreme from the Forth to the Tweed. He continued to translate woeful ballads from the German, but the idea of making money by his pen might never have occurred to him but for the lucky chance of his friend, Will Erskine, meeting the celebrated Mat Lewis in London. Mat had projected a miscellany, which would be the last word in skull-and-crossbones literature, and he was eagerly seeking contributors. When Erskine showed him the Bürger translations, the manikin's goggling eyes goggled and stuck out more than ever. Here was a man after his own heart. Would Mr. Scott contribute? Mr. Scott, flattered beyond expression, was only too glad.

> " Quod si me lyricis vatibus inseris,
> Sublimi feriam sidera vertice."

When presently the toy lion of Mayfair came to Edinburgh and actually invited him to dinner, he felt he need not repine at never having met Burns.

Fate has often made sport of momentous occasions by clothing them with ludicrous circumstances, but never more effectively than in this foregathering of two young men in an Edinburgh tavern. The picture—a great, heavy, rather countrified six-footer, with an oaken stick, limping up to receive a courtly greeting from an elegantly dressed creature of four foot something—is one which no pen need attempt. Only the comic pencil could do it justice. It is easy to laugh at " Monk " Lewis and at Scott for taking him seriously, but, apart from his freakish appearance, Lewis was no laughing matter in his own day. He had become a literary rage when he was barely out of his teens, and now, at the age of twenty-four—three years younger than Scott—he was the fashionable writer *par excellence* and a member of Parliament. Scott, who quite frankly regarded contemporary popularity as the grand test of literary merit, was bound to take such a personage seriously. Besides, he really liked the little creature, and the little creature was a good friend to him. Not long after the Edinburgh meeting Lewis placed Scott's version of Goethe's *Götz von Berlichingen* with a London publisher on terms which, if not great, were much better than Scott could have obtained himself. It was published in February 1799, and for the first time the name of Walter Scott appeared on a title-page.

To celebrate the event Scott and his wife went for a jaunt to London, where they were introduced to literary society under the distinguished auspices of Mat Lewis. Their enjoyment was broken into by the news that old Walter Scott had had another stroke and was sinking rapidly. But Scott still lingered in London. When a day or two later came word that his father was dead, he wrote to his mother in frigidly dutiful terms :

" The removal of my regretted parent from this earthly scene is to him, doubtless, the happiest change, if the firmest integrity and the best-spent life can entitle us to judge of the state of our departed friends. . . . The situation of Charlotte's health, in its present delicate state, prevented me from setting off directly for Scotland, when I heard that immediate danger was apprehended. I am glad now I did not do so, as I could not with the utmost expedition have reached Edinburgh before the lamented event had taken place. The situation of my affairs must detain me here for a few days more ; the instant I can I will set off for Scotland."

The deceased's estate was smaller than it might have been, but it was big enough to provide Scott with a welcome addition to his income. Before the year was out the " gentleman in a very precarious state of health " had the decency to die, and Walter Scott, Esq., advocate, was gazetted Sheriff of Selkirk, which would have been a great consolation to poor Walter Scott, W.S., if only he had lived to learn it.

II

In the autumn of 1804 there was no man in all Scotland happier than the young Sheriff of Ettrick Forest, and there were few that had more cause for happiness. He was just thirty-three—a splendid time of life. He had a pretty and much courted wife, a little boy and two little girls and ample means for their comfort and his own. That summer the death of his uncle, Robert Scott, had added £5,000 to his little patrimony. Parliament in a generous mood had lately raised shrieval salaries, so that his official position, besides being both dignified and easy, was not ill-paid.[1] His father being dead, the pretence of practising at the Bar was no longer a matter of obligation, but for social reasons he continued to attend at Parliament House until a plan he had for becoming a Clerk of Session should mature. Instead of the Lasswade cottage he had a country seat in Selkirk—Ashestiel, perched high above the Tweed —and he moved with modest assurance among the nobility and gentry of the Border counties. It is true that he had been very reluctant to leave Lasswade, which was conveniently near Musselburgh and the quarters of the Light Horse. Some people thought it was much too

[1] It was now made worth £400 a year.

near. One of these was the Lord-Lieutenant
of Selkirk, Lord Napier of Ettrick, who had
insisted with unpleasant emphasis that Scott's
commission as sheriff must take precedence
over his commission as quartermaster, that
there was a statutory obligation upon a sheriff
to reside part of the year in his sheriffdom and
that military valour must be tempered by
judicial discretion. Scott had protested that
the obligation was not always enforced, but
his lordship had been inexorable. It is
probable that he knew how the cripple lawyer's
hobby-horsical soldiering was being laughed at.
Otherwise Scott had little to complain of—
the death of Charlotte's first baby, perhaps,
and the sad case of young brother Dan, who
had to be shipped off to the Colonies for getting
a girl in the family way. Such paltry annoy-
ances are easily forgotten when one has the
great good things of life—youth, health,
strength, money, leisure—can ride hard, eat
hugely, drink deep and sleep like a log.

It was in these agreeable circumstances that
Scott began to consider literature as part of the
regular business of his life. As an apprentice
to the law he had dreamed of it, and as a briefless
barrister he had dabbled in it under the guidance
of Harriet Scott of Harden and Mat Lewis.
Now he could stand by himself. A respectable
London firm had issued two solid and well
annotated volumes from his pen, entitled *The*

Minstrelsy of the Scottish Border. The work, besides being highly praised, had made a profit that went some way towards compensating Scott for the time and money he had spent in collecting from oral tradition the ballads that formed the text. Since then he had published a revised edition, together with a third volume containing both genuine ballads and some experiments in the Scottish ballad manner by himself. There was one experiment, by far the most interesting and original, that he had not been able to include in the *Border Minstrelsy.* It was a long poem based on a Border goblin story and carried out in the metrical style of Mr. Coleridge's romantic fragment *Christabel* which he greatly admired. Owing to its length, which was far greater than he had ever intended, he had decided to publish this *Lay of the Last Minstrel* separately, and it was now in the press. He had a good, but perfectly just opinion of its merit as a competent and effective piece of work with enough novelty about it to make it popular. Mat Lewis's vogue had died a sudden and unlamented death. The public now wanted something better than second-hand skulls and crossbones from Germany, and Scott had a strong belief that he could supply the very article.

The first two volumes of the *Border Minstrelsy* had been brought out by Cadell & Davies, a good old firm that had published for Dr.

Johnson, but for a consideration they had disposed of their rights to Longman, Hurst & Co., who undertook the second edition and additional volumes. As a matter of course Longman, Hurst & Co. published the *Lay*. Associated with them in both ventures was Archibald Constable, one of the two men who were destined to rule the course of Walter Scott's life for good and evil, the other being James Ballantyne, printer, of whom more presently.

Constable was an even younger man than Scott, being just turned thirty, but his large and handsome personality was already looming up as a portent in the book trade, very much as the large and handsome personality of another young man loomed up in the newspaper trade a hundred years later. Alfred Harmsworth and Archibald Constable would provide a modern Plutarch with a parallel study that would extend even to physical characteristics. Both men had the fair, fleshy good looks that are often found with a restless, inventive and dominating spirit. Of the two Constable was the fleshier as he was the better-looking. Long before he was forty he was very fat indeed, but what he lost in symmetry he gained in majesty. He acquired so imperial an aspect that Scott, who had a nickname for everybody, dubbed him " the Czar," which pleased him, for he knew he had earned it. A mere yesterday it was since he had come from the East Neuk of Fife to be an apprentice in Peter Hill's bookshop in the High Street, where he had contrived to learn more about books and book-selling than his master, or even his master's master, old William Creech, ever knew. He had seen what the Edinburgh book trade amounted to, and it filled him with contempt—a few worthy bodies of mature years drowsing among dusty volumes that they had not the energy to catalogue and so indifferent to the publishing side of their business that when they did bring out a new book, it was never certain that the publisher's name would be on the title-page.

Yet all the time the potential market for books was increasing at an incredible rate. If ever an opportunity deserved the name of golden here it was, and Archibald Constable had marked it before he was out of his teens. He promptly made love to a prosperous printer's daughter, married her before he was twenty-one and started business on the proceeds. Within a few years the young Fifer was not only undisputed master of the trade in Edinburgh, but a force that the London booksellers had to reckon with. He was only twenty-eight when a plan for a new literary and political periodical was submitted to him by a young English clergyman then resident in Edinburgh, the Rev. Sydney Smith. Mr. Smith's plan was drafted on modest and cautious lines, but modesty and caution were not Constable's way. When he took up an idea he carried it out on the grand scale. He carried out the *Edinburgh Review* on the grand scale, and its immediate success was the reward of his courage and lavish expenditure. Without Constable's practical genius the united talents of Smith and his bright young friends Jeffrey, Brougham and Horner, could have produced no more than a brilliant but short-lived experiment. There is no reason to suppose that Constable's motives were disinterested. His business was to sell books and more and more books, and he believed in advertising. The primary function of the *Edinburgh Review* was to advertise the house of Constable. Its aggressive Liberal Whig politics were part of the scheme. The great new public that Constable had begun to tap were Liberals to a man.

Walter Scott admired Constable (who could not?), but he did not like him. "The Czar" was not the only nickname he had for him. There was another that Constable never heard —"the Crafty"—and it was grossly unjust. Constable was not in the least crafty. He simply had a real aptitude for affairs which Scott, not himself having, could not comprehend. That was one element in the antipathy. Another may have been that Scott could not quite stomach Constable's masterful behaviour towards those who had been born in better beds than himself. It is idle to press the analysis. The unfixed element remains. *Non amo te, Sabidi.* The situation was aggravated by Constable's partner, whom Scott cordially detested, though Alexander Gibson Hunter was a lawyer bred like himself, and even more a gentleman born, being the eldest son of the laird of Blackness in the county of Forfar. Mr. Hunter had paid handsomely for his partnership, and his special province in the firm was the counting-house, which the senior partner could never abide. He was a coarse, capable sort of young man, with an uncommonly good head for pounds, shillings and pence and strong drink. He also had a rough tongue and was proud of it.

We turn from Constable to the rather absurd little figure of James Ballantyne, an amiable nonentity who is remembered only because accident made him the measure of a great man's weakness. He was a Kelso shopkeeper's son, born in the same year as Scott. Their friendship had begun in boyhood during some fitful attendances that Scott had put in at Kelso Grammar School, and consisted of an affectionate patronage on the one side and a dog-like devotion on the other. Ballantyne had qualified as an attorney, but, like Scott, he had found law unremunerative and had turned in a humble way to letters. He owned a little printing business that produced the local Tory newspaper, the *Kelso Mail*. It was not a profitable venture, for no man who has not been brought up to the printing trade can hope to make money at it. What James Ballantyne had, however, was good taste and a real enthusiasm for printing as a fine art. Scott, who also knew the beauty of a well-printed page, was so struck by the excellence of Ballantyne's little press that he not only secured for it the contract for the printing of the *Border Minstrelsy*, but urged that it should be transferred to Edinburgh, where good printing just then was sadly to seek. Ballantyne hesitated. He had no capital. But Scott brushed aside all objections. He would provide all the money that was needed—it would not be much—and he could answer for the contracts coming in. Why, in official law printing alone he could get enough to keep the press going, and there were all sorts of possibilities and schemes to be worked out later—a really good Edinburgh newspaper, for example, and an *Edinburgh Annual Register*. These dazzling prospects, held out by so admired a friend, could not but prevail with a nature as facile as James Ballantyne's. The removal took place, and the last volume of the *Border Minstrelsy* was printed, not at Kelso, but in a dingy little shop in the precincts of Holyrood.

Poor James Ballantyne! It was no kindness thus to thrust greatness upon him. The position of a country printer and newspaper editor had been admirably suited to his powers and predilections, which were chiefly in the way of eating heartily and idling about with an air of importance. Now he was expected to manage a rapidly expanding metropolitan business which had been started on borrowed capital and far too little of it. Scott's promises of business had not proved false. Orders, including Longman's for the printing of the *Lay*, poured in at a rate that bewildered James not a little, but gave him a feeling of consequence. He moved to better premises in the Canongate, ate more than ever, and developed a droll pomposity of bearing that in time made him one of the standing jokes of the town. Scott laughed with the rest. He called him " Fatsman " and " Aldiborontiphoscophornio," cruelly apt nicknames for the obese little printer with the fruity *basso profondo* that delivered the lightest remarks in the diction of a stage tyrant, and the portentous grimace—one black eyebrow raised, the other lowering towards a dusky upper lip that was permanently screwed into a critical curl. These harmless foibles were the only defences that Ballantyne's simple honest soul could oppose to a world that was too much for him.

The New Year of 1805 was celebrated by the publication of *The Lay of the Last Minstrel* in a quarto volume that was a triumph of elegant typography. The first edition consisted of 750 copies. Before James Ballantyne could draw breath, he was labouring to produce an

octavo edition of 1,500, with every prospect
of more and more to follow. The *Lay* was
more than a success. It was a rage. Everybody
read it. It was the one topic of the day on
which the Prime Minister and the Leader of the
Opposition could agree. The great career of
the Wizard of the North had begun.

The young wizard was still in the glowing
contemplation of his first essay in enchantment
when his attention was drawn by certain
apologetic hems, and he turned to find at his
elbow the dark figure of his fat little familiar
Aldiborontiphoscophornio, who was in sad
perplexity. In choice and stately terms he
informed his master that he needed money and
a lot of it, and that if he didn't get it the press
would have to close down, which would be a
pity, seeing that business was so brisk. Scott
was utterly taken aback. In his innocence he
had imagined that if he provided for the
expenses of Ballantyne's removal to Edinburgh
and then saw that he had plenty of work to do,
all would be well. Neither he nor Ballantyne
had grasped the elementary truth that large
orders cannot be executed without commensurate
capital, and that if business increases faster than
reserves are built up one must get financial
support or go bankrupt.

Now that hard experience had made it horribly
clear, Scott was in a cruel predicament. Common
prudence told him that he ought on no account

to involve himself further with Ballantyne, and, if the application had come a little sooner or a little later, he could quite honestly have said that he had not the money. But just then, unfortunately, he had the money. There was the £5,000 realised from the sale of Uncle Robert's estate. He had intended to re-invest it in a more convenient landed property, but it was still lying loose in the bank. In the circumstances he could not absolutely say no to James. Was it not owing to him that James had exchanged his Sabine valley for the cares of the Canongate? Was he not bound in honour to see James safe as far as he had the power? Besides—and here the slumbering spirit of the moss-trooper became awake and alert—might not James Ballantyne's necessity be Walter Scott's opportunity for making easy money? Already, on a paltry advance of £500 and before his pen had found its power, he had put the Ballantyne press in a good way of business. If, as James said, a thousand or so would clear it of its temporary difficulties, what would a really substantial investment of capital not do? The pen of Walter Scott had a national reputation now, and whatever Walter Scott's pen wrote James Ballantyne's compositors could set. Why not? Scott suddenly took his fatal decision. He handed over his £5,000 in con- sideration of a one-third interest in the firm of James Ballantyne & Co.

The partnership was kept a dead secret, but the publishers who were now eagerly competing for Walter Scott's work remarked that the author would consider no contract that did not provide that the printing should be done by James Ballantyne & Co.

> " Oh, what a tangled web we weave
> When first we practise to deceive ! "

A more improper, a more dishonest, a more fatuous transaction it would be hard to imagine. Improper, because a commercial partnership was incompatible with Scott's position as a barrister, a judge and a prospective high official of the Supreme Court—hence the secrecy. Dishonest, because the publishers were never informed and, whatever their suspicions may have been, never supposed that Scott was actually taking profits as printer as well as author. Fatuous, because he thought it a sound speculation to pay £5,000 sterling for a one-third share in an insolvent business that would have been dear at £5,000 Scots. But Walter Scott just then cared for none of these things. Like Constable, though without Constable's sagacity, he realised that, for the first time in the long history of literature, there was money in the making of books. His head, humming with the wine of sudden success, was full of schemes, in all of which the chief feature was that they would provide Ballantyne & Co. with plenty of printing. Thus, if Constable or somebody would pay him thirty guineas a volume, he was prepared to edit, with exhaustive notes— biographical, historical and critical—a complete *corpus* of the British poets, from the earliest times to the present day, which was a *desideratum*. By the mercy of Providence nothing came of that, but William Miller, of Albemarle Street, was persuaded to pay forty guineas a volume for just such an edition of Dryden in eighteen volumes, which provided steady occupation for Scott's pen and Ballantyne's press for the next two years.

Any ordinarily industrious man, who had to perform the duties of an advocate, a judge and a hospitable country gentleman, would have found this task more than enough for his leisure, even if he had not in addition to perform the duties of a cavalry officer on quasi-active service —for in 1805 the bloody Corsican had newly crowned himself Emperor of the French, and 10,000 valiant men, securely encamped in Edinburgh, were bidding the tyrant do his worst. Yet Scott was able to cope with it all and much more. The Dryden, though respectable and laborious, was only superior hack-work. There were other things to do if the name he had made by the *Lay* was to be kept up—substantial and curious articles for the *Edinburgh Review* to be written, a new narrative poem to be thought about and foundations of a new kind of romantic novel to be laid. This sudden multiplicity of problems was attacked with a courage and address that can never be sufficiently admired. Haphazard work, however quick and diligent, could never accomplish what he now had in mind to do. There must be organisation—early rising, and at least three solid hours of desk-work before breakfast—and the raising of a corps of poor devils to look up references and copy extracts in the Advocates' Library. "Aye," he said many years afterwards, "it was enough to tear me to pieces, but there was a wonderful exhilaration about it all. I felt as if I could have grappled with anything and everything."

Towards the end of 1805 the plan to secure one of the Principal Clerkships of the Court of Session came to fruition. An aged incumbent was persuaded to retire on the handsome terms that he should continue to draw the emoluments of the office for life while his successor should perform all the duties. Some business connected with this appointment—the patent had not been drawn up in the proper form—took Scott to London in January 1806. The author of the *Lay* was duly lionised. He went to Hampstead to meet Joanna Baillie and to Blackheath to meet the Princess of Wales. To the latter place he repaired full of ardent sympathy for the poor victim of Whig malignity. He came away thoughtful. The Princess had tried to flirt with him.

In the spring he entered upon his duties as a Clerk of Session. Although as yet he could draw no salary—nearly six years elapsed before he touched a penny—he lost little by withdrawing from the Bar. For some time his only regular client had been his brother Tom, and that meant precious little, for Tom, whose talents were considerable for everything but business, was playing ducks and drakes with the remains of his father's practice. As the year drew to a close, and just as Walter was beginning a new metrical romance to be called *Marmion*, Tom failed. This was a heavy blow, for Tom was the Edinburgh agent of the Marquess of Abercorn, and Walter had guaranteed his fidelity. *Marmion* had to be tossed aside while the mess of Tom's affairs was cleared up. Everything that a generous and affectionate brother could do was done, but little financial assistance could be given, for Ballantyne & Co. had long since swallowed up the £5,000 advanced at the beginning of the previous year, and in addition had involved Scott in a heavy accommodation liability to Sir William Forbes, the banker who had married Williamina Stuart.

At this anxious juncture came Archibald Constable with a staggering offer. He was willing to pay a thousand guineas there and then for the copyright of the unfinished *Marmion*. There could be only one answer. Constable strode away in triumph. He had cut out Longman & Co. for the biggest prize of the day. Now the London publishers would know who was master. If any of them wanted a share in the venture, they would have to come to him, and they did. William Miller, of Albemarle Street, and young John Murray the Second (not yet of Albemarle Street, but coming on very fast), obtained a quarter-share each. *Marmion* was hastily completed. On February 23rd, 1808, it was published. In anticipation of a heavy demand an edition of 2,000 had been prepared, but within a month it was exhausted. Octavo editions followed in rapid succession.

While *Marmion* was in the first rushing tide of its success Constable discovered something that Scott had not seen fit to mention, viz. that he had recently engaged himself to a London firm to edit Lord Somers's *Tracts*. Constable was vexed. He had determined to have control of Scott's output, but " Earl Walter " was riding a very high horse now, and there was no dealing with him save by the persuasions of hard cash. Accordingly, swallowing his chagrin, Constable at once approached Scott with a proposal for an edition of Swift on the same lines as the Dryden that was now passing through the press for Miller, with this difference, that he was prepared to double Miller's price. He would pay £1,500 for it. The offer was promptly accepted. Constable felt that the future was assured. He and Scott, working together, could dominate the book world for a generation. They would in the course of nature die, but full of years and good wine and rich beyond the dreams of avarice.

O cæcas hominum mentes! O pectora cæca! This moment, when Constable was flinging gold at him with both hands and telling him that there was lots more where that came from, was the very moment that Scott chose to allow his smouldering dislike of the man to burst into flame. The trouble began with Jeffrey's review of *Marmion* in the *Edinburgh*. Due allowance being made for the fact that Jeffrey regarded himself as nothing if not critical—a conceit that often led him into silly fault-finding—it was a sincere and singularly acute judgment of the poem and of Scott's romanticism generally.

"To write a modern romance of chivalry," he wrote, "seems to be much such a phantasy as to build a modern abbey or an English pagoda. For once, however, it may be excused as a pretty caprice of genius ; but a second production of the same sort is entitled to less indulgence, and it imposes a sort of duty to drive the author from so idle a task, by a fair exposition of the faults which are, in a manner, inseparable from its execution. His genius, seconded by the omnipotence of fashion, has brought chivalry again into temporary favour. Fine ladies and gentlemen now talk indeed of donjons, keeps, tabards, scutcheons, tressures, caps of main-

47

tenance, portcullises, wimples, and we know
not what besides—just as they did in the days of
Dr. Darwin's popularity of gnomes, sylphs,
oxygen, gossamer, polygynia and polyandria.
That fashion, however, passed rapidly away,
and Mr. Scott should take care that a different
sort of pedantry does not produce the same
effects."

This was lofty, but an old friend should have
been more condoling. Scott was bitterly
offended. Yet by an extraordinary exercise of
unreason (to which Charlotte seems to have
contributed) it was not against Jeffrey, but
against Constable, that the Sheriff's main dis-
pleasure was directed, on the ground, apparently,
that he ought to have his dog under control.
Constable could fairly protest that the relation
of editor and publisher did not come within the
doctrine of *respondeat superior*, and that in any
case the dog's snappishness hurt the publisher
of *Marmion* more than it hurt the author, who,
after all, had had his money in advance. But
Scott nursed his grievance. The personal
question was aggravated by politics. His
Toryism had been intensified almost to fanaticism
of late, and so had the *Edinburgh Review's*
Liberalism. The same number of the *Edinburgh*
that had dealt with *Marmion* contained a political
article so uncommonly strong that John Murray,
when he read it, said, " Walter Scott has feelings,
both as a gentleman and a Tory, which these
people have wounded. The alliance between

him and the whole clique of the *Edinburgh Review*, its proprietor included, is shaken." He was quite right, but the alliance, though shaken, was not actually dissolved until six months later. The October number of the *Edinburgh* reviewed Scott's Dryden—very favourably, it is true, but with a suggestion that the editor's time and talents could be better employed than on glorified hack-work. The article was Hallam's, but Jeffrey got the blame. However, it was the Jacobinal puppy Brougham's outrageous article on the Spanish situation that was the last straw. In wrath too great for grammar Scott wrote to Constable : " The *Edinburgh Review had* become such as to render it impossible for me to continue a contributor to it. *Now* it is such as I can no longer continue to receive or read it."

Constable, his handsome face purpling with responsive rage, called for his list of subscribers and wrote against Scott's name " Stopt ! ! ! " Presently he heard that John Murray had arrived at Ashestiel on a mysterious mission. Before the year was out the High Street and Parliament House were buzzing with rumours of open war between Scott and his publisher. The *Edinburgh* was to have a Tory and Canningite rival, and there would be other developments for the chastening of Constable. One day Scott had a stormy encounter with the detested Alec Hunter. The junior partner was no respecter of persons. He would swear at a sheriff, or a Clerk of Session, or a fashionable author as readily as at a shop boy, and he told Scott that engagements with other publishers must wait until that damned edition of Swift was disposed of. Constable & Co. were paying a monstrous price for it, and would stand no nonsense. Scott told him to go to the devil, and then wrote a stiff letter to the effect that if Messrs. Constable & Co. rued their bargain he would be only too glad to release them. A grave and smooth reply came back. The senior partner was now speaking. Messrs. Constable & Co. by no means rued their bargain and meant to stick by it. Then would they be so good as to debit to Mr. Scott the cost of his portrait by Mr. Raeburn, which had been done to their order, and deliver it up to him? No, Messrs. Constable & Co. meant to stick by the Raeburn portrait also.

War was now declared. In the spring of 1809 John Murray published the first number of the *Quarterly Review*. It required no great acumen to remark that no fewer than three of the articles were from the pen of Walter Scott. "Aye," said Constable grimly, "there is such a thing as rearing the oak till it can support itself."

III

THE offensive against Constable consisted of
two parts. One, the starting of an opposition
review, which had been evolved by Murray
quite independently of Scott, was good. The
other, which was Scott's own idea, was not
good. Its essence was that Scott should be
not only his own printer, but his own publisher
as well. Not ostensibly, of course—that would
never do—but under a convenient cover. The
name of John Ballantyne, younger brother of
James, would serve, and Johnny could look
after the shop. The New Year of 1809, therefore, saw the opening in Hanover Street of a
smart new bookselling and publishing establishment that called itself John Ballantyne & Co.
Deep in the shady sadness of a safe, far sunken
from any healthy breath whatsoever, lay a
partnership deed setting forth that the " Co."
consisted of Walter Scott and James Ballantyne,
who each had a third share with John in the
concern—a curiously self-denying arrangement,
seeing that Scott (Heaven knows how) found all
the money. But the public saw only the gay
little figure of the nominal principal, who
greeted them with incomparable *bonhomie*.
Presently " our Mr. Ballantyne " was in London
conferring with John Murray upon the affairs

of the *Quarterly*, of which he had the honour
to be Scottish manager.

In the drama of Scott's life Johnny Ballantyne
appears as a tragic clown. He was a dear little
fellow, short like James, but as thin as his
brother was fat, having bad lungs, and he
had all the false brightness of the phthisical
temperament. His career had not, hitherto,
been prosperous. It had begun with a year
or two in his father's shop at Kelso, which
bored him. Next he had tried his luck in London, but after a few unhappy months as a clerk
in Currie's Bank he was glad to eat of the fatted
calf and become his father's partner. Next he
had quarrelled with his father and started as a
shopkeeper in Kelso on his own account. Next
he had failed, whereupon, seeing in adversity
the hand of Providence beckoning him to come
up higher, he had migrated to Edinburgh, and
fastened himself on his brother James. James
had obligingly installed him as chief clerk and
bookkeeper to James Ballantyne & Co. at £200
a year, which was far more than he had ever had
or was ever worth.

Now, in the firm of James Ballantyne & Co.
one partner was a lazy unbusinesslike creature,
and the other, for excellent reasons, had to keep
himself concealed. Here was an opportunity
for Johnny, and Johnny took it. He posed
as the business man of the firm, but not after the
Edinburgh fashion. He had been in the City

of London and knew better. He wore gay clothes of a sporting cut, hopped up and down the Canongate and High Street like a painted sparrow, chirping a waggish word here and a droll story there, and generally creating the impression of a man of the great world who carried his awful knowledge easily. It was his conceit to be "a great buck and a great beau," but there was a good deal of artfulness behind it. He was no exception to the rule that the man who sets up as a "character" is always slightly a rascal. Providence, however, in one of its kind but injudicious moods, has ordained that most of us should love rascals, and Scott loved Johnny Ballantyne, or "Rigdumfunnidos," as he called him. For Johnny was your perfect Yorick, a virtuoso in mimicry and jesting, whose like was not to be found in all Scotland, and when he gave his favourite *morceau*, "The Cobbler of Kelso," the Sheriff laughed till the tears rolled down his cheeks. But the histrionic temperament has its dangers in a world that is, unfortunately, not all a stage. Johnny's gift exerted itself in other concerns beside the legitimate business of entertaining. The smattering of banking lore he had picked up in London enabled him to extemporise brilliantly on the subject of finance, with special reference to accommodation bills, and Scott was deeply impressed. But as for capacity to manage an important publishing business that was to compete with the ablest mind in the trade, the first caddie on call in the High Street would have been, not merely as good, but a great deal better.

If there is one thing clear from Scott's private correspondence in the days of the *Lay* and *Marmion*, it is that he had no illusions about the nature of his success. He knew it for a bubble reputation. The only question was how big he could blow the glittering thing before it burst. The *Lay* had made his name and a tidy sum of money. *Marmion* had enlarged his fame and brought him a small fortune. Could he carry the popularity of the metrical romance any farther? He was sure he could, but he could not say how far. He judged, quite rightly, that his public would take a third, perhaps a fourth poem of the kind, and he had no doubt of his ability to deliver the goods indefinitely. But some day—a day not very distant—the impetus of novelty would fail. Another would supersede him even as he had superseded Monk Lewis. Yet at this dubious moment, when a prudent man would have reduced his commitments and taken his profit while the market was still good, Scott undertook fresh liabilities on a large scale and staked his whole future on the earning capacity of his pen. It was a dangerous, though not a blind gamble. He had something in reserve against the evil day—another romantic novelty that might be as astonishing and profitable as his

" light-horse octosyllables." He had often thought about this, had even experimented from time to time, but he agreed with Will Erskine and James Ballantyne—the only two intimates to whom the idea had been communicated— that the time for a new departure was not yet. And so a certain half-finished MS. was locked away in a drawer.

The firm of John Ballantyne & Co. was a failure from the beginning. Not a dismal failure, perhaps, for nothing could be called dismal that had " Jocund Johnny " in it, and it had a great moment of exaltation when its imprint appeared on the title-page of *The Lady of the Lake*. But that was in May 1810, when the firm had been in existence for eighteen months, during which time it had accumulated a dead-weight of failure that no single success could materially lighten. For this state of affairs the secret partner was chiefly to blame. His easy success combined with his native modesty to produce a curious conceit. He held —and posterity does not quarrel with his judg- ment—that his work had succeeded, not because it was good, but because it was what the public wanted at the moment. From that he argued that his *forte* was not so much that of a literary executant as that of a literary projector, from which it was an easy but treacherous step to conclude that any literary project that interested him would be certain to interest the public.

5   55

Against this delusion the Ballantynes were helpless, for Scott, in his own genial way, was exceedingly overbearing. He was the great man, and he knew it. They were men of straw, and they knew it. Hence the firm never had any publishing policy but Scott's whim of the moment. If, playing the part of the generous patron (which he loved), he chose to entrust a critical edition of Beaumont and Fletcher to a poor demented German who had been his amanuensis, or if, in an excess of pedantic patriotism, he proposed that Dr. Jamieson should write a voluminous *History of the Culdees*, the Ballantynes were in no position to withstand him. James, it is true, was often alarmed, for with all his absurdity he was at bottom a sane sort of creature; but he was too indolent and timorous to do more than bleat an occasional mild remonstrance which nobody heeded.

As for Johnny, who knew full well how the unsaleable stocks were mounting up, his one aim was to keep his job as long as possible. For the first time in his hapless career he was tasting, if not prosperity, at least some of the good things of life that are incidental to it, and he loved them with all the wistful eagerness of one who feels that he has not long to enjoy them. It was to his interest, therefore, that Scott should be humoured and kept in ignorance of the true state of the business. In this he was only partially successful. His artifices were too childish. When statements were required of him—and he irritated Scott by his reluctance to furnish them—they were invariably vague and disingenuous. Maturing liabilities would be concealed until they could be concealed no longer. Any evening the Sheriff of the Forest, making merry with his neighbours at Ashestiel, might be summoned from the festive board by the arrival of a courier with a frantic letter from Johnny. A matter of a few hundred pounds would be wanted to-morrow. Would Mr. Scott kindly sign the enclosed acceptance and return? The courier, having been suitably refreshed, would post back to Edinburgh with the bill and an indignant letter, and the Sheriff would return to his guests full of vexing thoughts. Johnny was not playing fair. Johnny was an unconscionable little wretch. Johnny owed everything to him, but instead of being grateful, treated his benefactor as a milch-cow. He would have it out with Johnny, wring the truth from him—the whole truth and nothing but the truth—and " age as accords." [1]

But somehow these stern decisions always evaporated when he came face to face with Johnny. The big lustrous, affectionate eyes, the droll mobile features, the ready jest, the blithe swagger of the poor wasted little body were too much for the good-natured Sheriff. He could no more be hard on Johnny than he

[1] Old-fashioned Scots lawyer's jargon for " take appropriate action."

could be unkind to dear old Camp or any of the other dogs that fawned about him at Ashestiel. Besides, after all, Johnny was useful in his way. He knew all about bills, and bills played an essential part in the precarious economy of the interlocked firms of John Ballantyne & Co., publishers, and James Ballantyne & Co., printers. Owing to the policy of the Scottish banks at that time, two firms, both being insolvent, and consisting of the same partners, could stave off actual bankruptcy by backing each other's bills. The fact that bills and counter-bills bore the same signatures made no difference. In the technique of these dangerous credit facilities John Ballantyne was an adept. He would put his name to bills not only with a light heart but with positive zest and *abandon*. On a fine morning his blue gig and smart tandem would drive up Hanover Street. Resplendent in blue coat and white cords Johnny would dart into the shop like a kingfisher. " Jock, ye b————r," he would bawl to his factotum, " fetch ben a sheaf o' stamps." Presently, having scribbled his name across half a dozen fateful slips of paper, the gay little bookseller would gather up the ribbons, crack his whip, and be off to the Musselburgh Races at a pace that was the admiration of the street urchins and the terror and scandal of godly citizens abroad on their lawful occasions. Walter Scott could not help loving such a man.

As if these business worries were not enough, fate ordered that at this time Scott should have family troubles of a kind peculiarly wounding to his pride. Dan Scott had come back from the Colonies in worse disgrace than ever. He had been overseer of a plantation in Jamaica. The niggers had mutinied, and Dan, the craven, had run away. He came home, a broken and dying man. Walter refused to see him or hold any communication with him. When he died, Walter dutifully wound up the affairs of his " unfortunate relative "—he would not call him brother. But he would not go to the funeral or wear mourning for him—the final gesture of anathema for a Scotsman of his generation and upbringing. In the course of his life Scott did many foolish and not a few inconsiderate things, but this was the only occasion of which it can be said that he behaved really ill. He was intolerant then because he was strong ; but many years afterwards, when he himself found that the back is not always fit for its burden, the ghost of poor Dan haunted him. The character of Conachar in *The Fair Maid of Perth* stands as his public repentance—" a sort of expiation to my poor brother's *manes*," as he put it to Lockhart.

If Scott was harsh to Dan, he was infinitely indulgent to his brother Tom, and from his anxiety to do that amiable but ineffective creature every possible good turn he found himself involved in a scandal which, though small, was sufficiently unpleasant while it lasted. As a Principal Clerk of Session he had the patronage of certain minor positions, and as Tom was necessitous he gave him a job. It was a very little one, but Scott's enemies noted two awkward circumstances—first, that the appointment had been made at a time when Scott must have known that the office was about to be abolished and that the holder would have to be compensated with a life annuity; secondly, that Tom Scott was not in a position to perform the duties of the office personally, the pressing attention of his creditors in Edinburgh having obliged him to reside permanently in the Isle of Man. The Parliament House Whigs shrieked with joy. They would "larn" Walter Scott to be a Tory jobber. Lord Lauderdale was primed to call attention to the scandal in the House of Lords. He was supported by Lord Holland, who wanted to know why Walter Scott should be petted and indulged by the party that had "shamefully neglected Robert Burns of glorious memory." When enough had been said to hurt Scott's feelings, the matter was allowed to drop, and poor Tom got his snip out of the taxes—£130 a year for life.

All these various worries were forgotten in the glorious triumph of *The Lady of the Lake*. Johnny Ballantyne, who had shrewd notions of preliminary puffing, had let it be known that

in his next poem Mr. Scott would unveil to the
British public the romantic beauties of West
Perthshire, which had the gratifying result
that, even before the date of publication, the
great tourist traffic to the Trossachs and Loch
Katrine, which is one of the staple industries
of Scotland to this day, had already begun.
When in due course *The Lady of the Lake*
appeared, the first edition—a handsome quarto,
done in James Ballantyne's best typography,
with an engraved portrait of the author by way
of frontispiece—was sold out immediately.
Four editions followed in rapid succession.
Within six months the sale had reached 20,000
copies. The reviewers vied with one another
in the popular task of laudation. It was noted,
as a curiosity, that Jeffrey in the *Edinburgh* was
even more cordial than Ellis in the *Quarterly*.
The public taste had been gauged to perfection.
The novelty of the scene, with all its wealth
of romantic suggestion, the exquisitely beautiful
heroine who never allows evil communications
to corrupt virginal good manners, the dark
and powerful villain, the gallant royal hero
travelling incognito, the juvenile lead of spotless
reputation—what more could the most exacting
public want? The title alone—a clever
reminiscence of Malory—was enough to guarantee success, and the text was worthy of it. The
Lay had delighted by its spontaneity; *Marmion*
was a capital story; but *The Lady of the Lake* had

charm, and nobody who has ever been to school will deny that it has it still. Kings may be blest, but Walter Scott was glorious. He was acclaimed on all sides as the greatest poet of the age. For the copyright of the poem his firm had paid him £2,000, and in addition as a partner, he was taking his share of the fabulous profits. It seemed to him that there was more money in the Highlands than in the Border. When he wrote his next poem there would be no stint of mountains and glens and clansmen and claymores. Accordingly, as soon as the Courts rose for the vacation, he was off to the Hebrides. The expenses of the trip were considerable, but being, as he argued, in the way of business, they were charged to the account of John Ballantyne & Co.

The mood of elation passed with the summer. Walter Scott came back to Edinburgh, to the routine of the Courts, to the interminable drudgery of his edition of Swift, to the anxieties of Johnny's shop and James's press, to a whole tangle of gratuitous tasks that his good nature had superadded to his obligations. In a few months his lease of Ashestiel would expire, and he had nowhere to go. A sudden nausea came over him. An interesting rumour about Lord Melville reached his ears and inspired a wild hope. " I have no objection to tell you in confidence," he wrote to Tom, " that were Dundas to go out Governor-General to India, and were he willing to take me with him, in a good situation, I would not hesitate to pitch the Court of Session and the booksellers to the devil and try my fortune in another climate." These words were written at Ashestiel in the month of November, and even at Ashestiel

> " November's sky was chill and drear,
> November's leaf was red and sear."

In Edinburgh the sky was as bad and the east winds were worse. The idea of " another climate " made a strong appeal. However, " new life revolving summer brings." When June came round Scott was again in high spirits. He had a new poem coming out—a romance in the Spenserian stanza. This in the ordinary course would have been a risky experiment; but as *The Vision of Don Roderick* was to come out in the name of charity, being the author's contribution to the fund for the relief of the victims of Masséna's campaign in Portugal, it was sure to be treated with the most delicate consideration. And in due course everybody was very polite about *The Vision*. George Canning, it is true, pointed out that the last line of the first stanza was too long by a foot, but that was a small matter. In a line so long as the Alexandrine an extra foot or two is neither here nor there.

There was another circumstance, far more fateful, that made the summer of 1811 memorable.

One morning in May Lord Melville was found dead in bed in his Edinburgh house. All thoughts of India had thenceforth to be abandoned. Scott's appointed place lay much nearer home, only seven miles from Ashestiel, in fact—a hundred acres of low-lying farm land, bleak and boggy, that could be had for £4,000. Scott fired to the idea of possessing it. He would be a Border laird in earnest. He would convert the poor farmhouse into a suitable "cottage," to be enlarged bit by bit until it should be a noble mansion, the glory of Tweedside. He would rename the place, even as Don Quixote renamed his hobby-horse, for its rustic name—Cartley Hole [1]—was obviously unsuitable for a gentleman's seat. Having anciently formed part of the lands of Melrose Abbey, it should henceforth be called Abbotsford. The only difficulty was that Scott had no money. The two Ballantyne ventures had not only devoured his capital, but were taking heavy toll of his income as well, and he was constantly puzzled by the curious circumstance that, although on paper he was making amazing profits, he never had a penny to spare. A little double-entry bookkeeping would have revealed even to his simple mind that in virtue of his engagements with the Ballantynes any payment he had for a copyright meant no more

[1] Not "Clarty," as Lockhart gives it. The perversion was probably deliberate. Lockhart was addicted to unseasonable facetiousness.

than a transference of money from a left-hand pocket to a right-hand pocket that had a hole in it. But as that never occurred to him, his first resource for the financing of the purchase of Cartley Hole was to use the machinery of the Ballantyne firms to obtain an advance of £2,000 on the security of a new poem that he had not begun to think about, much less to write. The other £2,000 he persuaded his elder brother, Major John Scott, to lend on mortgage.

It was a rash step, but not a reckless one, for he was about to have a very large addition to his income which would, he conceived, enable him to keep abreast of all possible obligations. As from January 1st, 1812, he would be in receipt of £1,300 a year as a Clerk of Session. A liberal superannuation scheme having been introduced, the ancient gentleman who had hitherto drawn the emoluments of the office had consented to retire. Scott felt secure. His clerkship, his sheriffdom and his wife's little fortune would bring him nearly £2,000 a year certain. For the rest he could rely on his trusty pen to gain some hundreds, even thousands, per annum—enough to satisfy all possible needs and not a few dreams. Before the year 1811 was out the purchase of Cartley Hole had been completed, and the Laird of Abbotsford—for so he was now greeted—was conferring with architects and builders.

It was in a complacent frame of mind, there-

fore, that during his last Christmas at Ashestiel
Scott turned over the plan of his new romance.
The Hebridean *mise en scène* upon which he had
lately spent so much time and money did not
appeal to him. In *The Lady of the Lake* he had
gone across the Highland line as far as Loch
Katrine (which is not now reckoned in the
Highlands), but beyond that he did not at the
moment care to venture. For like most Low-
landers of his time, he knew very little of the
Highlanders. Of their language, as he ruefully
confessed, he knew not a single word. Their
country he knew only in the cursory way of a
tourist. Their manners and customs he knew
only from books. On the whole it would be
more convenient to postpone the Hebridean
adventure and deal with something that had a
more familiar aspect, even if it was well on the
other side of the Border. He had a dear friend
in Teesdale, Morritt of Rokeby, whose domain
would make an excellent setting for a tale of the
Cavaliers and Roundheads. The local colour
would present no difficulty. In the ensuing
summer he would make a trip through the district,
and meanwhile he could appeal to Morritt for
some coaching :

" Is there not some book (sense or nonsense,
I care not) on the beauties of Teesdale—I mean
a descriptive work ? If you can point it out
or lend it me, you will do me a great favour,
and no less if you can tell me any traditions

of the period. By which party was Barnard Castle occupied? It strikes me that it should be held for the Parliament. Pray help me in this—by truth, or fiction, or tradition—I care not which, if it be picturesque."

"I care not which, if it be picturesque!" The spoiled darling of the public was growing very careless. A year later, when *Rokeby* was published, he was given a sharp reminder that public indulgence—he had already had it in full measure, pressed down and running over— is not limitless. The sales of *Rokeby* revealed that his market was breaking. Profits were there, but so diminished as to suggest that they were due, not to continuing motive force but to mere impetus, and Scott had the humiliation of learning from Tom Moore's *Twopenny Post-Bag* that the London wags had smoked his little game.

"Should you feel any touch of poetical glow
  We've a scheme to suggest.—Mr. Scott, you must know
  (Who, we're sorry to say it, now works for the Row),
  Having quitted the Borders to seek new renown,
  Is coming by long quarto stages to town,
  And beginning with Rokeby (the job's sure to pay),
  Means to do all the gentlemen's seats on the way.
  Now, the scheme is, though none of our hackneys can
      beat him,
  To start a new poet through Highgate to meet him;
  Who by means of quick proofs—no revises—long
      coaches—
  May do a few villas before Scott approaches;
  Indeed, if our Pegasus be not curst shabby,
  He'll reach without found'ring at least Woburn Abbey."

The charge of literary prostitution, now suggested with such galling facetiousness, was doubly hurtful. It was tolerably true and it was not new. It had already been made three years before in *English Bards and Scotch Reviewers* in terms that had made Scott, for the only time in his life, see as red as any Jacobin. "It is funny enough," he had written to Southey, "to see a whelp of a young Lord Byron abusing me, of whose circumstances he knows nothing, for endeavouring to scratch out a living with my pen. God help the bear if, having little else to eat, he must not even suck his own paws. I can assure the noble imp of fame it is not my fault that I was not born to a park and £5,000 a year, as it is not his lordship's merit, although it may be his great good fortune, that he was not born to live by his literary talents or success." But since then Byron had vanished from England, and Scott, like most people, had almost forgotten his existence when, in the spring of 1812, John Murray published the first two cantos of *Childe Harold*. The author's preface was curt almost to the point of insolence. "The scenes attempted to be sketched," he said, "are in Spain, Portugal, Epirus, Acarnania and Greece. There, for the present, the poem stops; its reception will determine whether the author may venture to conduct his readers to the capital of the East, through Ionia and Phrygia."

What could Scott do against a programme like this ? He had invented the poetical guide-book, but circumstances had confined him to " doing gentlemen's seats." *Cæteris paribus*, he could not compete with a noble lord whose means enabled him to " do " southern Europe and the Levant at his leisure and pleasure and who, moreover, by his perfect mastery of the Spenserian stanza showed a technical accomplishment that the author of *The Vision of Don Roderick* could never hope for. Yet Scott, though from the beginning he had known that one day the writing would appear on the wall, did not recognise it when it came. He was struck by *Childe Harold*; he could write to Joanna Baillie urging her to read it ; but he could not believe that a work so loose in moral tone could find acceptance. " It is, I think, a very clever poem, but gives no good symptom of the writer's heart or morals. . . . Vice ought to be a little more modest, and it must require impudence at least equal to the noble lord's other powers, to claim sympathy gravely for the *ennui* arising from his being tired of his wassailers and his paramours."

There was all the material here for a bitter literary feud, but John Murray's tact saved the situation. He wrote to Scott that Lord Byron had repeated to him some uncommonly flattering things that the Prince Regent had said about the most distinguished poet of the age, that his

lordship had associated himself with His Royal
Highness's encomiums, that his lordship was
evidently quite willing to let bygones be bygones
(which was very gracious of him) and that a
friendly letter to his lordship would be not
unwelcome. In a trice all Byron's insolence
and immorality were forgotten. After all the
young whelp was developing into a young lion.
Scott sat down at his desk and indited the
friendly letter. It was a painful exhibition of
clumsy obsequiousness, garnished with a verse
from Juvenal—"to let him see that I was a
scholar," as Dr. Primrose would have said—
and a postscript: "Will your lordship permit
me a verbal criticism on *Childe Harold*, were it
only to show that I have read his Pilgrimage
with attention? *Nuestra Dama de la Peña*
means, I suspect, not Our Lady of Crime or
Punishment, but Our Lady of the Cliff; the
difference is, I believe, merely in the accentuation
of the *peña*."

Byron, placing his tongue firmly in his cheek,
composed a civil reply. He declared on his
honour that Murray had not in the least
exaggerated the Prince Regent's opinion of Mr.
Scott's "immortalities." "He spoke alternately
of Homer and yourself, and seemed well ac-
quainted with both; so that (with the exception
of the Turks and your humble servant) you
were in very good company. . . . To be thus
praised by your sovereign must be very gratifying

to you ; and if that gratification is not alloyed by being made through me, the bearer of it will consider himself very fortunately, and sincerely, your obliged and obedient servant." Thenceforward, Scott would hear no ill of Byron. Three years later they met for the first time in John Murray's drawing-room. Changes had taken place. Murray had moved from Fleet Street to the historic house in Albemarle Street. Byron now wore the crown that had once belonged to Scott. Scott had conquered a new and greater kingdom, and envied no man. But in the interval he had had to endure much.

Rokeby was published in January 1813. Its failure was the opening calamity of a desperate year. Scott had confidently looked to it to provide some relief to the Ballantynes, whose difficulties had lately become a constant nightmare. That hope was gone now, and in addition the ugly truth was thrust in his face that his vogue was passing sooner than he had expected. Jeffrey, whose warning he had so sharply resented, had been wiser than he. The chalk was on his door and go he must. Awkward, yet a mere matter of readjustment. His pen would never fail him. There was the unfinished manuscript that for three years had lain unheeded in a drawer, and he could finish it in a few weeks. It was an undoubted novelty. The results might be surprising. But that was still future, and it was not the future but the

6 71

accursed present that made the problem. If he could not reduce his commitments with the Ballantynes drastically and promptly he was a ruined man, and it is the essence of a ruined man that he has no future. For the economic conditions of the year 1813 were such as terrified even the most solid business men. The Allies were in the throes of the final struggle with Napoleon, who at bay seemed more menacing and bloody than ever.

Great Britain was in a peculiarly evil plight. For all the blood and treasure that had been poured out in the Peninsula the issue was still in the earlier part of the year in doubt; the miserable war with the United States that had broken out in the previous year was still being waged; at home a starving and mutinous proletariat threatened revolution and terror. A griping scarcity of money and credit set in, and bankruptcies, even among firms that had been reputed good, increased rapidly. The two Ballantyne concerns were quite unfit to survive such conditions. It was obvious that in order to avert the collapse of both, the publishing business must be closed down. Nor was that the worst. To have to admit defeat is humiliating enough, but it is the very dregs of humiliation to have to ask your adversary for help. Scott found himself obliged to approach Constable. Fortunately the approach was not so difficult as it might have been. The personal quarrel had long since been composed. The obnoxious Alec Hunter had quitted the firm and retired to Forfarshire to nurse his gout and his estates. Constable now had as partners a Mr. Cathcart, who was a Writer to the Signet, and Mr. Cathcart's brother-in-law, a thin-lipped youth named Robert Cadell.[1]

Constable was sympathetic but wary. He showed no enthusiasm for the modest proposal that he should take over Scott's darling white elephant, *The Edinburgh Annual Register*, with its steady loss of £1,000 a year, but he was willing to buy a considerable amount of John Ballantyne's stock and a quarter-share in the copyright of *Rokeby*. Scott pleaded hard for a better offer, but " the Czar " had said his last word ; and the arrival of some of Johnny's long-dated bills reminded Scott that beggars cannot be choosers. The treaty was concluded. John Ballantyne & Co. got immediate relief to the extent of £2,000, and Constable promised to examine into the Ballantynes' affairs generally and advise as to the future.

That was in May. In August Constable made his report. It was bad. At least £4,000 must be forthcoming at once. If not—Mr. Constable raised his eyebrows. Could Mr. Constable help ? Mr. Constable pulled a sad face. He was afraid not, but Mr. Scott, with

[1] Robert Cadell was in no way connected with Scott's first publishers, Cadell & Davies.

73

his influential connexions, might possibly . . .
And so it proved. After a few distracting days
Scott could say that the Duke of Buccleuch
would back him for £4,000. The only question
was whether the relief had come in time. As the
autumn wore on and the Martinmas quarter-day
loomed up, the Ballantynes' distresses seemed
if anything to increase. Their bankruptcy was
expected hourly—was actually reported early
in November—and Scott, whose connexion
with the firms was notorious, though its true
nature was never suspected, was mentioned as
being involved to the extent of £20,000.

But the disastrous hour had not yet struck.
The month of October had seen the battles
of Leipzig and Vittoria. Napoleon had been
beaten to his knees. The war was virtually
over. Anxious traders could breathe again.
In the sudden revival of credit the Ballantyne
firms were saved—saved from ignominy at
least. John Ballantyne & Co., to be sure,
could not be continued as a going concern.
(Even Johnny conceded that and was now setting
up as an auctioneer of rare books, prints, and
articles of *vertu*—a calling for which he had some
real aptitude.) But it would be possible to
carry on until the stock had been disposed of
on reasonable terms.

Constable was master of the situation. The
whirligig of time had brought him his revenge,
but he was moderate, even generous, in his

triumph. If he had private thoughts about people who go out to shear and come home shorn, he was too judicious to give them utterance. If Walter Scott were bound to his chariot wheels, his chains should be of gold. Who could tell what wonders might ensue?

On February 1st, 1814, the *Scots Magazine* announced the early publication of *Waverly*, [*sic*] *or 'Tis Sixty Years Since*, a novel in three volumes. The author's name was not stated, nor was the publisher's. The latter detail was supplied, but not the former, when after some delay the book was brought out on July 7th by Constable.[1]

---

[1] In Edinburgh there could never have been any serious doubt about the authorship, for the July number of the *Scots Magazine* contained a long review which practically gave it away. The *Scots Magazine* had recently been acquired by Constable for the purpose of pushing his wares. The promptitude with which the review appeared and the fact that the misspelling of the title that occurs in the preliminary announcement is repeated throughout the review, except in the caption, suggest that the writer worked from proofs. The review ends with these words :

" Report assigns it to the most admired poet of the age ; a subject on which we have in vain sought for any information. The internal evidence does not certainly contradict the assertion ; and we see no reason that even such a writer could have to disown a performance like the present."

IV

In the spring of 1814 the Squire of Rokeby went to Paris and spent some time there. Immediately on his return he wrote to his celebrated friend, the Laird of Abbotsford, to inform him that the people of France were now sensible of the debt of gratitude they owed to the Allies, by whose disinterested (though hitherto misunderstood) efforts they had been at last restored to the incomparable blessings of Bourbon rule. He was in a position to speak with authority, having had the privilege of attending the first levee of "Monsieur," His French Majesty's amiable brother and heir-presumptive. This gratifying intelligence, though coupled with an intimation that Mrs. Morritt was not quite so well again, did not elicit the prompt reply that Mr. Morritt expected from a correspondent so punctual, so friendly, and so attached to monarchical and other sound principles. But at last, one day in July, there came from Edinburgh a letter and a small parcel. The letter said :

"I must account for my own laziness, which I do by referring you to a small anonymous sort of novel, in three volumes, *Waverley*, which you will receive by the mail of this day. It was a very old attempt of mine to embody some traits and manners peculiar to Scotland, the last remnants of which vanished during my own youth, so that few or no traces now remain. I had written a great part of the first volume, and sketched other passages when I mislaid the manuscript, and only found it by the merest accident as I was rummaging the drawers of an old cabinet; and I took the fancy of finishing it, which I did so fast that the last two volumes were written in three weeks. I had a great deal of fun in the accomplishment of this task, though I do not expect it will be popular in the South, as so much of the humour, if there be any, is local, and some of it even professional. You, however, who are an adopted Scotchman, will find some amusement in it. · It has made a very strong impression here, and the good people of Edinburgh are busied in tracing the author, and in finding out originals for the portraits it contains. In the first place they will probably find it difficult to convict the guilty author, although he is far from escaping suspicion. Jeffrey has offered to make oath that it is mine, and another great critic has tendered his affidavit *ex contrario*; so that these authorities have divided the Gude Town. However the thing has succeeded very well, and is thought highly of. I don't know if it has got to London yet. I intend to maintain my *incognito*. Let me know your opinion about it."

Such is Scott's own story of the origins of *Waverley*. It is repeated with more circumstance in the general introduction to the 1829 edition of the Waverley Novels. There is no

obligation upon anyone to believe it. It is,
in fact, untrue. A man of severely methodical
habits, who knows that every word he writes
has a cash value and who is in dire straits for
money, does not forget the existence of a
considerable piece of work, and Scott had not
forgotten *Waverley*. The idea had occurred
to him in the autumn of 1805, and seven chapters
were written forthwith. Will Erskine, the only
person to whom he confided everything, did
not like them much, so they were set aside.
A year later they were brought to mind by a
letter from Robert Surtees of Mainsforth, a
learned and ingenious Northumbrian squire,
who had once amused himself—being in a poor
state of health—by inventing ancient ballads
and passing them off on the unsuspecting com-
piler of the *Border Minstrelsy*. Surtees wanted
to know why Scott did not write something
romantic about Prince Charlie. Scott acknowledged that really he must do something
of the kind, but he was silent about what he
had done. In 1808 James Ballantyne could
hint to John Murray that Scott's bag of tricks
contained a startling novelty that would be
produced when the time came. In 1810, having
been reproached by Surtees for not yet having
done anything towards writing " la très piteuse
et délectable histoire du preux et errant Chevalier
Charles Stuart," he wrote a few more chapters
and submitted them to James Ballantyne, who,

while more cordial than Will Erskine had been, nevertheless counselled delay. It is not easy, therefore, to believe in the "merest accident" by which the author, searching for some fishing tackle, lighted upon the unfinished manuscript among his old junk. That pleasant fiction must be relegated to its proper place as part of the curious system of mystification in which Scott persisted for the next thirteen years.

He had recently tried his hand at the game and found it amusing. Only two months after the publication of *Rokeby* the Ballantynes issued a modest-looking volume entitled *The Bridal of Triermain*. It was a short narrative poem in the new romantic manner. In a scholarly, not to say ponderous, introduction the anonymous author professed to be no more than a humble disciple of Walter Scott, and proceeded, with the aid of one quotation from Diogenes Laertius and another from Herodotus, to a disquisition on the difference between epic and the so-called romantic poetry, " the popularity of which has been revived in the present day, under the auspices, and by the unparalleled success of one individual." George Ellis, who reviewed *The Bridal* for the *Quarterly*, was most egregiously taken in. Edinburgh—with the exception of Francis Jeffrey, who saw at once that the thing was Scott's—speculated wildly about the authorship. Some said it was by the crack-brained dilettante Robert Pearce Gillies, but these were not the best-informed people. The best-informed people were able to say positively that it was the work of Will Erskine; and as that mild and learned gentleman did not deny the attribution, the point was regarded as settled. But before long the success of *The Bridal* became a little embarrassing to the putative author; and when a third edition was called for, poor Will, who at the beginning had been a ready enough accomplice, protested that the joke was going too far for his taste, and obliged Scott to avow his authorship.

With the *Bridal* hoax still fresh in the public memory, it is surprising that Scott should have attempted another prank of the same sort, and on a more elaborate scale. The reason he always professed—that *Waverley* was a dark horse, and that he could not afford to have his name associated with a failure—cannot be treated seriously. At no time was he averse from taking even the greatest risks, and in the case of *Waverley* he was taking no risk—at least he thought not, for he demanded an exorbitant price for the copyright. He simply wanted to be mysterious—it was his humour. He even tried to hoodwink Constable, which was quite unnecessary for his professed purpose. But the natives of Fife are not noted for their simplicity. This one smiled at the Border Sheriff's transparent artifices, and offered £700 for the copyright of *Waverley*. Never before had such terms been offered for a work of fiction, but they were rejected. The author stuck out for £1,000. After some haggling it was decided that *Waverley* should be published on half-profits.

When the Court rose for the vacation Scott was full of glee. He was going off on a great and glorious holiday—a voyage round Scotland as the guest of the Northern Lights Commissioners—having just made arrangements with Constable for a second and larger edition of *Waverley*. In the three weeks that had elapsed since publication the first edition was almost exhausted. Six joyous weeks more and Scott was back in Edinburgh, his face glowing with the salt winds, the sun and the rains, his whole being on fire with the wonders of the Orcades and Hebrides, and his next poem, *The Lord of the Isles*, as clear in his head as the stiff price he meant to get for it. In Edinburgh he found Constable awaiting him all in a fret. A third edition of *Waverley* must be put through the press at once, and probably a fourth would be needed before the year was out. Would Mr. Scott be agreeable to continue on half-profit terms? Mr. Scott, hugging himself delightedly, was quite agreeable. (Aha! "the Crafty" had overreached himself for once. How sick he must be that he had not bought *Waverley* outright for £1,000!) And now, in Constable's firm impressive accents, came an inquiry about the new poem, *The Lord of the Isles*, as he understood it was to be called—a most attractive title. As Mr. Scott was aware, he was prepared to pay 1,500 guineas for one-half of the copyright, which Mr. Scott must agree was a very large sum ; but after the most careful consideration he could not agree to the condition, upon which Mr. Scott had hitherto insisted, that he should also take over a large quantity of Mr. John Ballantyne's stock, which frankly he did not consider a highly marketable commodity. Scott, in his present good humour, could not find it in his heart to haggle. The bargain for *The Lord of the Isles* was struck. The poem was completed in the autumn and was through the press by Christmas.

Yet, with it all, the Laird of Abbotsford was hard put to it to " keep his Christmas merry still." It had been gratifying in a way to find that Francis Jeffrey, while respecting the anonymity of the author of *Waverley*, was not deceived. The new departure was greeted in the *Edinburgh* with the same detachment and the same virile appreciation as had been accorded to *Marmion* and *The Lady of the Lake*. It had been amusing also to note that, although John Murray evidently knew what was what, he had kept his own counsel to the extent of allowing Croker to damn *Waverley* in the *Quarterly* with all the ignorance, ill-temper and imbecility of which that talented personage was capable.

But those were small compensations for Scott's present discomforts. His extemporised cottage at Abbotsford was draughty and inconvenient. Bills accepted by Johnny Ballantyne continued to mature with alarming frequency. Charles Erskine, his sheriff-substitute, whom he had induced to invest £500 in John Ballantyne & Co., wanted his money back in a hurry. "Would to God I were let-a-be for let-a-be," wrote the Sheriff to Johnny, "but you have done your best and so must I." His best was to write in the six weeks of the Christmas vacation a new novel "by the author of *Waverley*," which Johnny was authorised to dispose of to any publisher who would deal on a half-profits basis, advance £1,500 and take over £500 of Ballantyne rubbish.

Despite the marvellous success of *Waverley* the publishers were not attracted by these terms. Constable would not look at them. John Murray shook a dubious head, and Blackwood behaved no better. In the end it was from the house of Longman that *Guy Mannering* was put forth in the last week of February 1815.

By that time Scott knew that his course as a poet was run. *The Lord of the Isles* had come out in January. He had hoped and believed that it would be another *Lady of the Lake*, but the first returns from the booksellers were even more disappointing than those of *Rokeby*. Clearly the Harp of the North was beginning

to pall on the public ear. The minstrel gave
a little gasp of dismay and promptly tossed the
instrument upon the shelf. It had won him
many a golden guinea; but he candidly admitted
that its strains were provincial compared with
the exotic modes of *The Giaour,* *Lara* and
The Bride of Abydos, and perhaps his fingers
were not as supple as they used to be. No
matter. He could still tell a stirring tale better
than any man alive. *Waverley* was in its fifth
edition, and *Guy Mannering* was already selling
like hot cakes. The new line looked like being
even more lucrative than the old. The work
was easier, the market bigger and steadier,
and there was no one who even pretended to be
a competitor. In the course of his life Scott
had often been favoured with brilliant prospects,
but never had his glimpses of the morrow been
so glorious and golden as they were in the
spring of 1815. Even the news of the Corsican
bandit's return from Elba could not disturb
him. Only another novel or two and all would
be clear. The slow and vexing winding up of
Ballantyne & Co. would be honourably completed. The plans for Abbotsford would not
be hindered. He felt justified in giving some
indulgence to his guilty appetite for acres.
There were some desirable little adjoining
properties that could be acquired.

Anyhow, he could afford an immediate trip
to London with Charlotte and Sophia, who was

now twelve. The little girl saw a great deal of London—all of it, in fact, on a clear day, for she stayed with Miss Joanna Baillie at Hampstead, and a stone's throw from Miss Baillie's garden on Windmill Hill there was a place that commanded a complete prospect of the great city. It was just past the tavern, and the assembly-room, and the funny little house where, as Miss Baillie could well remember, Mr. Romney used to live. Mr. Romney was a great painter, but Mr. Raeburn in Edinburgh, who had painted Papa's portrait, was just as great. Papa and Mamma were stopping with Mamma's old friend, Miss Dumergue, who lived in Piccadilly. Sometimes they would come out to Hampstead by coach and take Sophia into town, and she would learn all about Papa's doings, which were wonderful. He had not only been presented to the Prince Regent, but had been commanded to dine at Carlton House. Also he had at last met the celebrated Lord Byron at Mr. Murray's house, and the two had become so friendly that they saw one another nearly every day; but except that he was lame, like Papa, and very, very brilliant, Sophia did not gather much about his lordship.

Truth to tell, Scott never knew quite what to make of Byron, and was never really at ease in his company. He always had the feeling that his successful young rival's temper was as uncertain as his principles in politics and religion.

The Prince Regent was a much more comfortable personage. He arranged " snug little dinners " for Scott at Carlton House, capped funny stories with him, and always called him " Walter." Of course His Royal Highness would sometimes have his little joke. Once he had called for a bumper, with all the honours, to " the author of *Waverley*," but Walter was not to be caught napping ; he drank the toast, and cheered with the rest, whereat His Royal Highness had smiled, and immediately proposed the author of *Marmion*. By the end of May the Parliament House gossips were able to hear of these pleasant doings from Scott's own mouth, and some were allowed to see the jewelled snuff-box that testified to His Royal Highness's affectionate regard.

The eventful year went on. Waterloo was fought. Six weeks later Walter Scott was on board the Harwich–Helvoetsluys packet *en route* for Brussels and Paris. He must needs see the field of battle and write a poem about it forthwith for the benefit of the widows and orphans of the glorious dead. He also saw a chance of making a few hundred guineas by rushing out a short book of personal impressions of what was going on in Brussels and Paris— unblushing journalism, but too profitable to be despised. In Paris, thanks to the kindness of Lord Castlereagh, Lord Aberdeen and Lord Cathcart, he was handsomely entertained, gazed on an astonishing number of sovereign princes and even spoke with some of them. The story of how the Sheriff pulled the Czar's leg was a prime favourite in Parliament House for many a day. He came home through London and saw Byron once more, and (as it proved) for the last time. It was not such a happy meeting as in spring. Scott, full of his charity poem, had only one subject of discourse, but Byron did not seem to kindle to Waterloo. He yawned, and even sneered in a very wounding way at Scott's moving anecdotes of heroism. (He remembered them when he came to write the second part of *Childe Harold*.)

Late in the autumn Scott set to work on his third novel. He had agreed to let Constable have it, but he would be thirled to no man's mill, and if in future " the Czar " did not show himself more accommodating about taking over quantities of John Ballantyne's stock as part of the bargain, the author of *Waverley* could easily make other arrangements. He was afraid of no man alive—always excepting the Duke of Wellington, who could make the boldest feel like a delinquent schoolboy—and he who could face Czar Alexander Romanoff could surely face Czar Archibald Constable. Let " the Crafty " look to himself . . .

But meanwhile *The Antiquary* must be written.

V

At seven o'clock on a November morning Edinburgh is yet some distance from anything like daylight, so the elderly-looking gentleman who sat at his desk in a back room in Castle Street in the year 1822 worked by candlelight. He was a very large gentleman with a red, weatherbeaten face and untidy white hair. These and other particulars of his personal appearance were much in his mind at the moment. The frown of concentration relaxed and the long upper lip flickered slightly with amusement as he wrote rapidly in a small neat hand :

" The Author of *Waverley* entered, a bulky and tall man, in a travelling greatcoat, which covered a suit of snuff brown, cut in imitation of that worn by the great Rambler. His flapped hat—for he disdained the modern frivolities of a travelling cap—was bound over his ears with a large silk handkerchief, so as to protect his ears from cold at once and from the babble of his pleasant companions in the public coach from which he had just alighted. There was somewhat of a sarcastic shrewdness and sense, which sat on the heavy penthouse of his shaggy grey eyebrows—his features were in other respects largely shaped, and rather heavy than promising wit or genius ; but he had a notable projection of the nose, similar to that line of the Latin poet

    ' immodicum surgit pro cuspide rostrum.'

A stout walking-stick stayed his hand—a double Barcelona protected his neck—his belly was something prominent, ' but that's not much ' —his breeches were substantial thickset—and a pair of top-boots, which were slipped down to ease his sturdy calves, did not conceal——"

Sir Walter Scott, Bt., paused for a moment to snuff the candles and resolve positively that Abbotsford would not be perfect without a handsome installation of the new gas lighting— not coal gas, but the superior illuminant provided by the Edinburgh Oil Gas Company, of which he was chairman. Candlelight was too dim for ageing eyes that had still much to do. The library and study at Abbotsford—these were still to be built, but at last he had the architect's plans—must be well lighted. He would have a good strong jet of oil-gas over his desk. It was wonderful what a gallon of the basest train oil could be made to do : modern advances in science and invention were all wonderful. Sir Humphry Davy was a great man—nearly as great as the Duke of Wellington —and Sir Walter had met them both. Even the Bramah pen was a wonder compared with the old quill.

"——did not conceal his comfortable travelling stockings of lamb's wool, wrought, not on the loom, but on wires, and after the venerable ancient fashion——"

Looms, weavers, Radicals! Confound all rogues and traitors who would not be content with the venerable ancient fashions. The Border, which should have been the very sanctuary of eld, was a hot-bed of sedition, though, thank God, the Sheriff of Selkirk knew what his duty was and had dealt faithfully with all such rascality, with the result that in the Forest at least the mechanics were imbued with sound principles and thoroughly contented.

"——the venerable ancient fashion known in Scotland by the name of *ridge-and-furrow*."

Ridge-and-furrow! A symbol of the life of man. The ridge was always followed by the furrow and the furrow by the ridge—that had been his experience for more than twenty years, and probably would be for another twenty, if he lived so long. He was fifty-one now, but he knew that he looked and moved more like sixty. He must put the best face on it.

"His age seemed to be considerably above fifty, but could not amount to three-score, which I observed with pleasure, trusting there may be a good deal of work· had out of him yet; especially as a general haleness of appearance— the compass and strength of his voice—the steadiness of his step—the rotundity of his calf—the depth of his 'hem,' and the sonorous emphasis of his sneeze, were all signs of a constitution built for permanence."

A constitution built for permanence! He earnestly hoped and prayed it might be so, but during the past few weeks there had been things that made him doubt—queer feelings in the head and occasional falterings of memory that were disagreeably suggestive of apoplexy. He feared they had left some mark on the novel he had just completed—his sixteenth in eight years.

An hour or so later Sir Walter laid down the Bramah pen, glanced over what he had written, folded the manuscript into a packet and sealed it up. It was the Prefatory Letter to *Peveril of the Peak*—a light morning's work, a mere *parergon*. He enjoyed writing these prefatory letters. They had been begun and continued as part of the *Waverley* mystification. That joke was wearing thin now, but it had become part of his life and he could not bear to give it up just yet, even if it was a *secret de Polichinelle*. Everybody must know what had made the Prince Regent offer Walter Scott a baronetcy just after the publication of *The Heart of Midlothian*, and likewise what had enabled Walter Scott, not only to accept so expensive an honour, but also to maintain its dignity at Abbotsford with a magnificence that was the talk of all Scotland. But apart from the fact that he enjoyed it, mystification had proved too good an advertisement to be dropped, and the detailed self-portrait prefaced to *Peveril* was but a new phase. He could no longer keep people from wondering who the author of *Waverley* was, but he could keep them wondering what Walter Scott's motives might be in refusing to admit what he was at no pains to conceal.

He rose, gathered up the reference volumes that lay on the book-tray beside him and, limping painfully about the room, returned each to its place among the sleek folios and quartos that covered the walls from floor to ceiling. He resumed his chair to await the breakfast hour. . . .

No, he had not been very happy over *Peveril*. That was partly because the book was ill-planned to begin with. He would avoid that mistake in the next novel, which would be about a Scots archer in the French King's guard *tempore* Louis XI. (How he loved the fifteenth century!) On the other hand, everything, even getting up and sitting down, had become more difficult of late, and he had the deepening awareness of mortality that is the common experience of the closing years of middle-age even when health is unbroken. And Walter Scott had had a serious illness. One evening in the spring of 1817, in the middle of a dinner-party at Castle Street, he had uttered a sudden scream of agony and fled from the table. He was suffering from

gall-stones. For two years, with varying inter-
missions, the attacks recurred. Opium was
needed to get him through *Rob Roy*. For *The
Heart of Midlothian*, luckily, he had a peaceful
interval, but *The Bride of Lammermoor* was a
horror—a delirium of pain, with little Rigdum
dimly remembered as taking down from his
dictation words that were forgotten as soon
as uttered. He had been very near death in
those days, and when he rose from his sick-bed
his hair was white and the foundations of life
seemed rather less solid than of yore ; yet through
it all his output of work had been maintained.
For eight years he had averaged two novels
a year, and even now he saw no reason why
(God willing) he should not do the like for
seven years more, which was well, for he could
not afford to stop writing yet. Exactly how
much the novels brought him he could not say,
for the payments made to him formed part of
a tangle of bill transactions with Constable and
James Ballantyne & Co. that only an expert
accountant could have unravelled. All that he
could be sure of was that it was an amazing
deal of money—at least £10,000 in the best
years and never much less than £8,000—and
that he was spending every penny of it.

But there was another aspect of the matter.
It is true that Scott in 1822 could not have stopped
writing even if he would. It is equally true
that even if he could he would not. His work

was not merely a necessity but a consolation, a refuge from the instant sadness of life, which his spirit demanded, no matter how loudly his flesh might cry,

" parce, precor, precor—
non sum qualis eram."

For the human scene was changing with fell rapidity. He and Tom were now the only survivors of their family, and poor Tom (who had escaped from his embarrassments by becoming an Army paymaster) was in Canada. John, the half-pay major, had died in 1816. Old Mrs. Scott, having lived to see her famous son a baronet, departed in peace three years later. The cantankerous Robert and the invalid Anne were fading memories, though the scapegrace Dan's reproachful shadow seemed rather to gather substance with the years. These were saddening thoughts, yet they did not strike at what with Walter Scott were the very issues of life—the friendships of his youth and manhood. Within the last eighteen months he had lost the two men whom he had worn in his heart of hearts. Johnny Ballantyne was the first to go —Jocund Johnny, who gasped out piteous little quips between his hemorrhages, and, optimist to the end, used his latest breath to tell his dear friend and patron that, as a small token of gratitude, he was leaving him £2,000 towards the completion of the great library at Abbotsford, as to the arrangements of which he was proceeding to give some valuable hints when a paroxysm of coughing brought the doleful interview to a close. A few days later Scott stood by his grave in the Canongate churchyard. " Where be your gibes now ? your gambols ? your songs ? your flashes of merriment that were wont to set the table in a roar ? " As for the £2,000 legacy, that had been poor Johnny's latest joke, though he never knew, for his whole estate proved to be worth considerably less than two thousand pence, and Scott and Constable had had to concert some provision for the widow.

In that melancholy autumn of 1821 it had been a welcome distraction to bustle about, seeing people and writing letters, so as to get Will Erskine made a judge, which he fully deserved to be and might have been long ago if he had had a little more brass on his brow. A happy day came in the New Year when Scott, from his place at the Clerks' table, beamed affectionately on the spectacle of gentle Will in Court dress timidly presenting his commission as a Senator of the College of Justice and taking his seat with the judicial style and title of Lord Kinedder. But Will, with his exquisite sensibility and feeble body, was quite unfit for such a position. A few months of judicial life made him a nervous and physical wreck. Then someone set afloat a *fama clamosa* about him, coupling his name with a woman's. It was a lie, as fatuous as it was malignant, but

it was more than Will Erskine could bear, and
he took to his bed. Scott was very full of
affairs just then, being master of ceremonies
for the visit with which George IV was about
to honour Edinburgh; but he was daily at
Will's bedside, doing his best to console and
cheer. It was all in vain. One August morning
Scott, arrayed in ceremonial tartan, rode down to
Leith, bewildered by the emotions of grief and
exultation that strove with each other in his
breast. The pageant of Scotland he had devised
for the Royal visit was in perfect order. The
noblest of the Highlands and the Lowlands had
(not without persuasion) submitted to be his
obedient mummers. The Castle guns crashed
out their welcome to the King. But Will
Erskine had died that morning.

However, the Royal visit was a great success.
There were grumblers, no doubt, who hinted
that Sir Walter was taking a great deal too
much for granted and seemed to think that
Scotland was spelled with two t's. There
were serious people to whom the elaborate
display of tartans and claymores savoured of
play-acting, a thing in itself deplorable, but
doubly so when it referred to ancient vanities
"tending rather to shame than to honour."
There were young Parliament House gigglers
—and not all of them were Whigs, either—who
paid an ironic tribute to the genius of the man
who could prevail upon the First Gentleman

in Europe—being sixty years of age and sorely incommoded by his belly—to put on a kilt and hope that some good might come of it. But Scott, though he heard of these things, cared for none of them. For him there had been but two tiny flies in the precious ointment of the occasion. One concerned his costume. His only strain of Highland blood came through a great-grandmother who was a Campbell; hence, said his antiquarian conscience, he must wear the Campbell tartan or none at all. As the latter was not to be thought of, Scotland had the curious pleasure of seeing the hierophant of sentimental Jacobitism wearing the livery of Whiggism in order to pay his respects to a Hanoverian prince clad in the tartan of the House of Stuart. However, that was a trifle.

The other matter was much more vexing. Scott had dashed off a new version of the old Jacobite song, " Carle, now the King's come," brimful of hilarious loyalty and really, for an occasional poem, very well done. But by an evil chance the idea of " new words to an auld spring " had also occurred to a Radical weaver in Glasgow, Sandy Rodger by name. This lewd fellow, " timorem Dei non habens ante oculos, sed suadente Diabolo," published his verses simultaneously with Scott's, and as they began

> " Sawney, now the King's come,
> Kneel and kiss his gracious b——,"

and proceeded to various facetious allusions to His Majesty's private morals, they were found to have a popular appeal that Sir Walter's loyal effusion somehow lacked. That such a thing should be possible made Sir Walter for a moment blush for his country. Presently, however, he was able to set off against the seditious indecency of the Glasgow weaver the gratifying fact that Edinburgh bailies had better table-manners than London aldermen. No doubt His Majesty would note that, whereas the Coronation banquet had been a disgusting scramble for victuals and drink, the Edinburgh civic banquet was a model of decorum. When all the turmoil was over, the master of the pageant was well content. It had been a great personal triumph for the author of *Waverley*. He had for a few days realised the Scotland of his dreams ; and having secured the King's promise that the peerages forfeited in the Fif-teen and the Forty-five should be restored and that Mons Meg should be returned to Edinburgh, he felt he had deserved well of his country.

These were pleasant things to remember. They helped him to forget—and he hoped they helped other people to forget—the exceedingly unpleasant things that had immediately preceded them. If Heaven could have blotted out the year 1821 from his life Walter Scott would have been a much happier man, for he had been de-tected in a course of conduct that he had neither the effrontery to defend nor the grace to repent. The growing unpopularity of Liverpool and Castlereagh and the turbulence of the new Reform agitation had so wrought on the nerves of the Scottish Tories that they were in a mood for any folly. They started a weekly paper called *The Beacon*, which in virtue of its vulgar personal abuse of prominent Whigs soon enjoyed a considerable circulation among judges, advocates, writers, ministers of the Gospel and others of the more respectable sort of Edinburgh people. In especial its scurrilities were directed against Mr. James Stuart, of Dunearn, and Mr. James Gibson, W.S. Mr. Stuart, a simple laird, could think of no better remedy than to catch the printer of *The Beacon* in the High Street and give him a public caning. Mr. Gibson, being a lawyer, was more subtle. He wrote to the Lord Advocate, Sir William Rae, charging him with being art and part in the disgraceful business. His Lordship's reply was " sicuti Mons Meg crackasset"; for to the consternation of everybody, he coolly admitted that *The Beacon* was being financed by himself and—Sir Walter Scott and a few more, all honourable men ! Mr. Gibson had no wish to take extreme measures, even if they had been feasible—for after all one cannot call out His Majesty's Advocate—and he was satisfied by Sir William's assurance that he had no responsibility for *The Beacon* save as a guarantor of its finances. Could Sir Walter Scott give a like assurance ? Sir Walter could, but he would be hanged if he would for any Whig alive ! The consequence was that one day he had a call from Lord Lauderdale, who explained that he had come on behalf of his friend Mr. Gibson, and would be glad to have the name of a gentleman who would act on Sir Walter's behalf.

But that duel at any rate was never fought. Thoroughly frightened, Scott's friends interfered. He was persuaded to give the required assurance, in which the other guarantors joined. *The Beacon* was abruptly discontinued. Scott's humiliation was complete. The disclaimer of personal responsibility that had been extorted was true only by the card, as he well knew. Old friends looked askance at him and received with chilling silence his protestations that he had been dragged into the affair against his better judgment. They knew that, if he had not inspired, he had openly countenanced the scurrilities of *The Beacon*, which would soon have ceased if the young Tory hotheads who wrote them had not been able to count on Walter Scott's laughter and applause. Nor was that all. Although *The Beacon* had been extinguished, the flames of party rancour burned as fiercely as ever, and Scott had reason to feel not only humiliated but alarmed. " I expect daily to hear that somebody is killed," he wrote to Constable at the end of 1821. Four months later somebody was killed.

The Beacon's libels on Stuart of Dunearn had been renewed with even greater virulence in *The Sentinel*, a Glasgow newspaper of the same discreditable sort. They were traced to Sir Alexander Boswell, of Auchinleck. Stuart and Boswell met at Auchtertool in Fife on March 22nd, 1822. Boswell fell. Some weeks earlier he had been Scott's guest at Castle Street in the highest spirits, rivalling even his host in conviviality and exuberant anecdotage. The horrid shock of his death suggested to Scott a naïve and mournful conclusion. " I begin to think," he wrote to Maria Edgeworth, " that of the three kingdoms the English alone are qualified to mix in politics safely and without fatal results ; the fierce and hasty resentments of the Irish, and the sullen, long-enduring, revengeful temper of my countrymen, make such agitations have a much wider and more dreadful effect amongst them."

Even life was conspiring with death to increase his melancholy. He had undertaken marriage at what is regarded as the ideal age for a man— young, yet not too young—and the reward of his discretion was that now, when he was entering his fifties, life was claiming his children as death was claiming his friends. For years, at a cost that in money alone he hardly dared to reckon, he had laboured to build on Tweedside as Kubla Khan did by the sacred river. He was immensely proud of Abbotsford's turrets and what he was pleased to call its " queer old-fashioned archi-

tecture." But there was no nursery at Abbotsford. Even Charles, the youngest child—he
had been born at Ashestiel—would soon be
going to Oxford. Walter, the heir, was a
subaltern in the 15th Hussars, which had meant
a heavy capital outlay as well as a liberal allowance. He was now improving such mind as
God had given him—his father sometimes felt
that God had been rather unhandsome in that
regard—by means of Continental travel, which
also was expensive. Sophia, the elder girl,
was married. Her husband, Mr. John Gibson
Lockhart, was an advocate, but did not practise
much, preferring literature. He was a very
talented young man, had been to Oxford,
travelled on the Continent and met Goethe, and
his political principles were faultless. Sir Walter
Scott had a high opinion of Mr. Lockhart. The
young couple lived on the Abbotsford estate and
had a little boy now a year old, who was a great
delight to his grandfather.

Anne was still a maid. She was a good girl,
sensible, affectionate and spirited. Sir Walter
would have been glad to see her well married,
but on the whole he was more glad to think that,
inasmuch as her good qualities did not include
good looks, such an event was unlikely. For
the distaff side of the Scott household was in a
precarious condition. Poor Charlotte had never
been much of a manager, and now, what with
her asthma and her bad heart and her difficult

time of life, she was really incompetent. If Anne were to go, Abbotsford would be virtually without a mistress, and its master would be a very uncomfortable as well as a very lonely man. Almost Scott was tempted to envy James Ballantyne, who, marrying late in life, was now the doting and ridiculously fussy father of a small family. And thereby hung a tale.

When Fatsman, first ensnared in love, approached the lady of his affections, a Miss Hogarth, she referred him to her brother. That was in 1816. Mr. Hogarth, an attorney and a prudent man, could not forget that the Ballantynes had lately had the narrowest possible escape from bankruptcy. He was very insistent, therefore, that James should satisfy him that he was now free from liabilities. This was reasonable, but awkward. There was only one way out of the difficulty, viz. that James should cease to be a partner in the firm that bore his name and become a salaried manager instead. The arrangement satisfied Mr. Hogarth, Fatsman got his bride and Scott became sole partner in James Ballantyne & Co.

But when on that November morning in 1822 Scott directed the last of the *Peveril* copy to Mr. James Ballantyne, the position had again changed. After five years as manager Fatsman was a partner once more, and the taking of accounts that had been necessary when the change was made had revealed a state of affairs that gave Scott a feeling of compression at the heart. However, he would manage somehow, barring a breakdown in health. He was surely good for a few years yet. And there was a brighter side to things. Whatever his present commitments might be, he was quit of the shabby borrowings from friends which had poisoned his earlier career. The kind Duke of Buccleuch, who had come to his aid in 1814, was dead, alas ! But he had lived long enough to receive back his bond for £4,000 discharged. *The Heart of Midlothian* had paid for that. It was some comfort, too, that even if the worst came to the worst the children were safely provided for, seeing that their uncle, Charles Carpenter, who had recently died in India, had left them the reversion to his considerable fortune. And Abbotsford, whatever people might say, was a solid asset. . . .

Sir Walter Scott thrust the packet of copy into his pocket and extinguished the candles, for it was now daylight and breakfast was ready. He was always very hungry for breakfast. At ten o'clock he would be in his place in Parliament House. Men junior to him were being promoted to the bench, but he was still drudging at the Clerks' table. Once or twice there had been talk of him having, not a Court of Session judgeship but a Baron's robe in the Scottish Exchequer Court, which would have suited him very well. But nothing had come of it. After all, what did it matter ? A judgeship might ease things

slightly, but it would not release him from the
necessity of turning out copy for "the Crafty."
But there—even the Devil must have his due,
and so must Archibald Constable. In the matter
of advances for unwritten novels Constable had
been very liberal. Of course he knew on what
side his bread was buttered, but all the same his
behaviour was handsome. In those days the
author of *Waverley* almost liked his publisher.

VI

ARCHIBALD CONSTABLE believed in being handsome. It was his business faith, and his friend, the author of *Waverley*, lost no opportunity of putting it to the test. For two years or so after the crisis of 1813 Scott had been very strict with himself, paying off debts with all diligence and averting his eyes from seductive parcels of land. But with the discharge of the Duke's guarantee came a dangerous liberation of spirit, and an orgy of land purchase began. Like the drunkard, Scott had his repentant moods when he would tell himself that the latest purchase must positively be the last, but the craving was always too strong for him, and presently yet another addition would be made to his acres at whatever price the vendor had chosen to ask for it. At the same time the building of Abbotsford had to be provided for, and it was proving much more costly than he had expected. It thus came to pass that, in spite of the profits of the novels, he was repeatedly in dire straits for large sums of ready money, and it was always to Constable that he looked for assistance in raising them. He never looked in vain.

The assistance was given in three ways—purchase of copyrights, advances on new novels and bank accommodation. The first purchase of copyrights was in the year 1818, towards the end of which Scott's occasions were so urgent that he decided to sell out all his existing literary property, lock, stock and barrel. Constable bought them without demur at the author's figure—£12,000. For the next three years the output of Waverley Novels was enormous and the profits were likewise. One memorable twelve-month (1819–20) produced *Ivanhoe*, *The Monastery*, *The Abbot* and *Kenilworth*. These four novels alone brought Scott more than £10,000, yet by the end of 1821 he was asking Constable to let him have 5,000 guineas for the copyrights, and in addition to make large advances for four new novels that could not even be named in the contract because the author's fertile brain had still to conceive them. Constable was agreeable. Owing to the magnitude of the sums payment was made, not in cash, but in bills of longish date. These liabilities, large as they were, caused him no anxiety. The copyrights were value received, and the advances on unwritten novels, though they constituted a risk, were covered by an insurance policy on Scott's life.

The case of bank accommodation was different. Constable was not so easy about that. From 1816, when he became sole partner in James Ballantyne & Co., Scott had been in the habit of using his firm's credit for his personal convenience—that is to say, he borrowed money by making bills in the name of James Ballantyne

& Co, getting Constable & Co. to back them,
and in return giving Constable James Ballantyne
& Co.'s acceptances for like amounts. These
transactions represented no value, and the
security created by the counter-bills was quite
artificial. Scott, in fact, so far from profiting
by the sharp lesson he had had in 1813, was continuing and developing the financial system of
Johnny Ballantyne and involving Constable in
its perils. When in 1821 James was taken back
into partnership the balance-sheet then struck
showed that although the firm had been making
steady profit on trading account, Scott had
saddled it with a debt of £30,000 in respect of
advances to himself. The bulk of that debt
consisted of accommodation transactions with
Constable & Co.

If Constable was uneasy, his junior partner—
he had only one now, for Cathcart was dead—
was much more so. Robert Cadell was not of
the handsome persuasion. Meticulous and calculating, always cool and clear-headed except
in an emergency, he often found it hard to work
with a daring and ingenious man who would
never allow an end to fail for lack of means.
For a young man of gentle birth he was remark-
ably sensible of cash values. Having on more
than one occasion tried Constable's handsome-
ness on the balance-sheets he had found it wanting. In the case of Scott, of course, he knew
that it was not disinterested, that its purpose—

a purpose that had in the main been achieved—
was to keep the author of *Waverley* away from
Murray and Longman, and he was far from
denying the worth in prestige and money that
accrued thereby. On the other hand, he knew
that the firm, though big and prosperous, was
not yet really rich. It had suffered a serious
reduction of capital by the death of Cathcart,
and its credit, though excellent, had quite enough
to do in supporting Constable's ambitions without the additional burden of financing Scott's
extravagances. Accordingly Cadell lost no
opportunity of urging upon his senior the importance of caution in all his dealings, especially
his dealings with Sir Walter Scott.

In pressing for sound finance Cadell had a
double interest. He was Constable's son-in-law
as well as his partner, and it was on a family
matter that the inevitable quarrel broke out.
Constable had aged even more rapidly than
Scott. For a comparatively young man—he
was still in the forties—he was far too fat and
florid to be healthy, and in the spring of 1821
he became definitely ill. One day he informed
Cadell that he was making his will and proposed
to name Sir Walter Scott as one of his trustees.
This was too much for Cadell. It seemed to
him that Constable's regard for Scott had passed
from a business policy into a personal infatuation.
He protested angrily that, in view of Sir Walter's
heavy engagements with the firm, such an ap-

pointment would be grossly improper. Constable could not, or would not, see that. An embittered struggle followed which lasted for months. It was only by Cadell finally threatening a dissolution of partnership, which would have meant a sudden and ruinous withdrawal of capital, that Constable was brought to yield. The quarrel was composed, but the partnership was permanently weakened.

A year passed. Scott's floating debt was larger than ever, and Constable was finding cause to feel very serious indeed about it. He hated the sight of a balance-sheet, but he had a loving and discerning eye for sales-returns, and he noted that the *Waverley* curve had reached its peak with *Ivanhoe* and was now definitely tending downwards. The idea that Scott's popularity was declining could be dismissed at once. All the evidence pointed the other way, and even the critics agreed that he was writing as brilliantly as ever. Only one inference was possible—that the novels were being produced faster than the market could absorb them. The rather cool reception that *Peveril* had from press and public decided Constable. He would not discourage Scott with talk of diminishing returns and glutted markets; and by the same token it would be inadvisable to raise the question of debt reduction just yet; but he would propose a new literary project to be undertaken at once and long and laborious enough to secure that there should be no more novels written for the next two years. An elaborate edition of Shakespeare would answer very well. It was a desideratum; it would pay; and it was the kind of temptation that Scott could never resist. He broached the idea to Cadell, and once more the partners were at odds, for Cadell could see no sense in it.

The junior partner's argument had that hard simplicity which is conclusive rather than convincing. The firm, he said, had paid out large sums for novels that had still to be written— questionable business, but there it was, and they must make the best of it. So far from staying the production of novels they should speed it up and get quit of their engagements with Scott at the earliest possible date. The market might be showing symptoms of glut, but it was not yet glutted, and profits were profits, even if they were diminishing. It would be a very risky thing to divert Scott's activities from fiction. He might die in the middle of the Shakespeare, or the public taste in fiction might change. A hundred things might happen. Clearly Constable & Co.'s motto for the moment should be " small profits, quick returns and get your money back while you can." On the other hand, Cadell agreed that if Scott were willing to part with the copyrights of his last four novels (including *Quentin Durward*, which was now passing through the press) they should be acquired. This was done, coupled with the intimation that no more propositions for novels could be entertained for the present. When *Quentin Durward* was published a few weeks later Constable found his fears confirmed with disconcerting emphasis, for though a far better story than *Peveril*, it sold even worse. The *Waverley* situation was getting out of hand. Constable & Co.'s bill commitments with Scott amounted to £60,000, nearly half of which consisted of mere accommodation and only about one-third represented value actually received.[1] Accordingly, in August 1823, Sir Walter Scott had a long letter from Messrs. Constable & Co. politely but particularly inviting his attention to the matter of his floating debt and the reduction thereof to a reasonable figure—say £8,000—within the next few months. He replied that he would make the necessary arrangements.

And straightway *Quentin Durward* confounded every calculation. The author of *Waverley* was suddenly discovered by France. France went mad over him : Germany and Italy followed. This miracle-worker, who had never quitted his native shores but once—when he made his hurried trip to Brussels and Paris—had produced a picture of Louis XI and his age that at a single stroke gave him an ascendancy in European literature that was and will remain unique. His

---

[1] The actual figures were: copyrights, £22,500; advances on unwritten novels, £10,000; accommodation, £27,000.

equipment for the *coup d'état* had consisted of Comines's *Memoirs*, a French gazetteer and a map of Touraine.

Scott was gratified, of course, but not specially elated, for he did not yet realise his new honours, and in any case his mind was preoccupied with a richer satisfaction than all the literary triumphs in the world could give. Save for a few finishing touches Abbotsford was complete. When all was done it would have cost him one way and another between £70,000 and £80,000, at least half of which had still to be earned by his pen ; but he reckoned that, provided his vogue held (which it looked like doing) and his health did not absolutely break (like Constable's), he would, by the time he was sixty, be free of debt and have a few bawbees to leave the bairns when he went to his long home. *Quentin Durward* was certainly cheering. It proved that he need not be bound to British soil for the scenes of his romances. There was no need to envy the errant Byron now. Provided there was some sort of book about a place, Walter Scott could go anywhere without the expense of leaving home. For his next novel he fancied Germany, and some day (as the ingenious Constable had suggested) the curious history of Sir John Hawkwood would be a good excuse for invading Italy. And there was no reason why he should stay in Europe either. He could follow his old and profitable friend Richard Cœur de Lion into

Palestine, explore Virginia with Captain John Smith and Pocahontas . . . Verily God was blessing him as He had blessed Jabez—by enlarging his coast. However, on second thoughts he decided to postpone foreign adventures for a little. He had written nothing about Scotland since *The Abbot* and nothing about contemporary life since *The Antiquary.* " Hame's hame, be it never so hamely," said he as he addressed himself to *St. Ronan's Well.*

The floating debt was forgotten.

VII

CONSTABLE, too, was seeing new horizons and meditating new conquests. Scott's crowning triumph had come at a peculiarly happy moment. In spite of industrial unrest and political agitation trade had recovered from the post-war depression and was now improving at a great rate. During the year 1824 nothing seemed to be so easy as the making of money, and when 1825 opened commercial enterprise was running riot in all kinds of commercial speculation. New joint-stock companies sprang up every day, and the produce markets were disorganised by gambling transactions on the part of strangers who had no knowledge of the commodities in which they purported to deal. Constable was not infected by the general folly. Daring he was, but not reckless; a bold adventurer but never a gambler; always prepared to take great risks, but always knowing the reason why. Again and again he had shown that his apparent audacity was merely the courage of superior insight.

At the same time he was not the man to stand idle in the market-place while other people were busy on Tom Tiddler's ground. The speculation fever, he knew, would pass—pass calamitously, perhaps—but the rapid increase of the nation's

real wealth, which it betokened, would continue.
The fools would be ruined, but the wise men
would go on growing richer, and among the
wise Constable with justice included himself.
But at this point he made a curious discovery.
In his own time and owing largely to his own
enterprise and example, the book trade had
expanded enormously and made unprecedented
profits, from which it was natural to infer that
it was getting its fair share of the new wealth.
But calculations based on the annual schedule
of assessed taxes revealed the fact that, whereas
the nation's luxury spending had reached a figure
that even a generation earlier would have been
deemed incredible, the book trade was getting
hardly any of it. People were spending their
money on fine houses, on costly furniture, on
servants, on horses, on delicate food and drink,
on gadding about—on luxuries of every des-
scription, in fact, except books. Constable was
astounded. Here was he, the cleverest man in
the trade, worth £100,000 if he was worth a
penny, and for thirty years he had gone on without ever, so to speak, doing more than scratch
the soil! Well, soon he would change all that.
He had made one revolution in the publishing
trade, but it would be nothing to the revolution
he had in mind now—always provided that
Walter Scott would help him and medical skill
keep his heart going for a year or two more.
The working out of a scheme did not take long.

In the first days of May its general features were confided to young Mr. Lockhart, who was to convey them to his father-in-law and report. Mr. Lockhart reported that Sir Walter had pronounced it "the cleverest thing that had ever come into that cleverest of all bibliopolical heads" and was very earnest to discuss the whole matter in detail with Mr. Constable.

Next Saturday, accordingly, the meeting between the two great men took place at Abbotsford in solemn form, Mr. Lockhart and honest Sancho Panza Ballantyne in attendance. The Sheriff was in the best of spirits. Evidently this was to be a famous year. It had begun most auspiciously. All through Christmastide the halls of Abbotsford had rung with high revelry in honour of the approaching nuptials of the heir, which were duly solemnised in February. True, the bride's name was Jobson, "yet that's not much" compared with a large property in Fife, and she was not ill-looking. The match had been of Sir Walter's own contriving, and young Walter—"desiderato acquiescens lecto"—had behaved like a good boy. It was a proud father who, in terms of the marriage settlement, subscribed the deed that entailed Abbotsford on his elder son. "I have now parted with my lands," he exclaimed, "with more pleasure than I ever derived from the acquisition or possession of them"—a sentiment that was a thought exaggerated for a common form transaction that made no difference to him whatsoever, seeing that he retained the life interest and the right to charge to the whole estate up to £10,000. But he went on to the really warming reflection, that with ten years more of active life and reasonable literary luck he would be able to double his settlement on the young folks ; and now here came Constable with a scheme that promised to turn his hope into a certainty.

He drank his whisky-and-water and smoked his cigar while Constable expounded the great idea, telling the Sheriff—and the Sheriff, nodding seriously, said he was very right—that the last thing a moneyed man thought of possessing was a library. " But if I live for half a dozen years," he said, " I'll make it as impossible that there should not be a good library in every decent house in Britain as that the shepherd's ingle-nook should want the saut-poke. Ay, and what's that ? " he went on with labouring breath and his face flushing with emotion to a deeper crimson. " Why should the ingle-nook itself want a shelf for the novels ? "

The Sheriff took a sip of whisky and screwed up his lip. " I see your drift, my man," he said. " You're like for being Billy Pitt in Gillray's print—you want to get into the salt-box your-self."

The reply came with a bang on the table. " Yes, by God. I have hitherto been only thinking of the wax-lights, but before I am a twelve-month older I'll have my hand on the tallow."

The Sheriff's mouth stiffened with appreciation. This was Napoleonic, and he said so. The imperial bookman, gracefully acknowledging the compliment, proceeded to business.

" May I presume to ask you to be my right-hand man when I open my campaign of Marengo ? I have now settled my outline of operations—a three-shilling or half-crown volume every month, which must and shall sell, not by thousands or tens of thousands, but by hundreds of thousands—ay, by millions ! Twelve volumes in the year, a halfpenny of profit upon every copy of which will make me richer than the possession of all the copyrights of all the quartos that ever were, or will be, hot-pressed ! Twelve volumes so good that millions must wish to have them, and so cheap that every butcher's callant may have them if he pleases to let me tax him sixpence a week ! What do you say to taking the field with a Life of the *other* Napoleon ? "

Scott could have wished for nothing better. It was there and then arranged that the first number of *Constable's Miscellany* should be the first half of *Waverley* and the second number the first of four volumes of a *Life of Napoleon Bonaparte* by the author of *Waverley*. A few weeks later, when all plans were ready, Constable wrote to his London agents, Messrs. Hurst &

Robinson, who now for the first time heard of the *Miscellany*. As their reply came by return of post he broke the seal fully assured in his expectation of their enthusiastic assent. But instead he was met by an angry demand. Did he want to ruin them, they asked, by flooding the market with cheap reprints of the Waverley Novels while large stocks of the existing editions remained on hand? They insisted that the *Miscellany* should be abandoned forthwith. Constable was furious. An acrimonious correspondence went on all through the summer and into the autumn. It ended in a compromise, sulkily enough agreed to on both sides, by which the *Miscellany* was to proceed but was not to include the Waverley Novels.

Early in October Constable went to London. Hurst & Robinson's opposition to the *Miscellany* had puzzled as well as angered him. He could not afford to break with them, for they had always been very obliging about backing his accommodation bills, and in return he had often backed bills of theirs, a matter which caused him no concern, as their financial resources were large—much larger than his own. That cheap reprints of the Waverley Novels would injure the sales of existing editions he did not admit—on the contrary he believed it would improve them—but even if it did, the loss would not be ruinous to a firm of Hurst & Robinson's standing. Was their agitation not

simply that panic that invades conventional dull
minds at the first glimpse of anything novel or
bold ? There was this excuse for them, that the
money market had lately taken on an ugly look,
and the banks had become regular Shylocks
about discounts. Heaven, Constable reflected,
had played him a shabby trick by sending the
idea of the *Miscellany* just when the financial
weather began to break. When the Abbotsford
conclave met there had already been some signs
of a change of wind, but nothing to worry about.
In June, when he wrote to Hurst & Robinson,
the sky towards the City was threatening. In
October it was black, and casual adventurers
were scurrying to cover before the storm broke.
These considerations suggested another possi-
bility. Was there—could there be—anything
wrong with Hurst & Robinson ? Of late they
had been drawing on Constable & Co. for
accommodation as never before—to an extent
indeed that was just a little awkward for the
firm's credit. But no, the notion was absurd.
The houses of Hurst & Robinson and Constable
& Co. could withstand any storm. Their
foundations were secure. A few slates off the
roof—that was the worst that could happen.

Yet in the atmosphere of Paternoster Row
Constable found nothing but deepening perplexity. It was true that Hurst & Robinson
proved amenable to his persuasions about the
Miscellany, but they coupled their complaisance

with a pressing request for financial assistance on a biggish scale. It appeared that they were committed to certain speculative dealings which, of course, would be highly profitable in the end, but were in the present state of the money market embarrassing. In his hotel in the Adelphi, between the copious but not too alarming letters he wrote to Cadell, Constable pondered anxiously. He was in the common enough mercantile dilemma of being involved with a firm that he could not afford to support and dared not allow to fail. Of course, if the worst came to the worst he must pawn his shirt for Hurst & Robinson, but he could not bring himself to believe that things had or could come to such a pass. On the whole, he concluded that Hurst & Robinson would be able to weather the storm without his help and so he informed them.

While these discussions were proceeding in London, Scott at Abbotsford was working as even he had never wrought before. His ardour and copiousness in the matter of Napoleon had caused the original plan of a short book for the *Miscellany* to be abandoned in favour of an historical work in the grand manner, which, in view of the amount of research involved, would have been regarded by any other man as ample work for a lifetime. Materials, printed and in manuscript, arrived at Abbotsford in carts by the load, but they were read and digested so

rapidly that early in October Scott was calling
out for more. To fill in the time of waiting he
began a new novel, *Woodstock*. He felt very
tired but also very happy, the only vexation being
that much poring over the files of *Le Moniteur*
had lately obliged him to take to spectacles.
His business affairs had ceased to oppress him.
When he had a little leisure he would straighten
them out and regularise the situation with
Constable, but meanwhile he refused to worry
about what was largely a question of bookkeeping that could easily wait. It was wonderful
that at his time of life he should be entering
upon a new phase that promised to be the most
prosperous of all. When he looked out at his
beloved Tweed and the trees of his planting he
called to mind the upright man of the First
Psalm. How went the Vulgate? " Tanquam
lignum quod plantatum est secus decursus
aquarum." But the metrical version was yet
more comfortable to a Scottish heart :

> Which in his season yields his fruit,
>   And his leaf fadeth never :
> And all he doth shall prosper well. . . ."

Certainly Providence was smiling on the
family. The year, which had begun with Walter's
most desirable marriage and his promotion to
a captaincy (price £3,500), had now in its fall
brought John Murray's astounding and gratifying proposal that Lockhart should become

editor of the _Quarterly_ in place of Mr. Coleridge,[1] who had made a very indifferent successor to Gifford. Lockhart was even now in London arranging his contract, which one way and another would be worth £3,000 a year. Scott wrote him long letters full of good advice about the deportment proper to an editor of the _Quarterly_, the sum and substance of which was that he should on no account be seen in the company of Theodore Hook. Lockhart on his part reported that the negotiations were proceeding smoothly to their conclusion. That was good hearing. But he also took it upon himself to report various items of City gossip, as, for example, that the book trade generally was in a bad way owing to the collapse of speculation, that in particular Hurst & Robinson had made a disastrous gamble in hops and might be in the _Gazette_ any day; and that City men looked down their noses when Constable's name was mentioned. Scott frowned, not with anxiety, but with annoyance that Lockhart should have thought absurdities so palpable worth paper and ink. Granted that the money market was bad and that weak firms might go under, it was difficult to believe that any serious harm could befall a firm like Hurst & Robinson; while as for Constable, Scott had no hesitation in assuring

[1] John Taylor Coleridge, afterwards Mr. Justice Coleridge of the Queen's Bench and father of Lord Coleridge, C.J., had succeeded Gifford in the previous year.

Lockhart by return of post that, whatever might happen to others, Constable was "rooted and branched like an oak." Having delivered himself of this comfortable rhetoric he dismissed the matter from his mind and went on with *Woodstock*. In the last week of October Lockhart arrived home from London, and in his new quality of editor of the *Quarterly* received his affectionate father-in-law's congratulations and blessing.

One evening some ten days later Archibald Constable's travelling equipage drew up before his house at Polton on the Great North Road, six miles from Edinburgh. The master descended painfully, thanked his sons for their supporting arms and went to bed. He was a sick, exhausted man. For a fortnight he lay in agonies of gout, breathlessness and anxiety about the money market. His last journey to London looked like being his last indeed—but no, by God, it should not. He had no time to waste on thoughts of death, with a crisis approaching that he alone had wits and courage enough to cope with. Anxious he was, but not downcast, nor was he the man to allow bodily weakness to quell his spirit. He directed his business from his bed, receiving Cadell's daily reports and dictating—for he was unable to hold a pen —long and precise instructions in reply. Day after day went by, bringing neither comfort nor actual bad tidings. Advices from London continued to be gloomy, but Hurst & Robinson's credit was evidently holding well enough.

But at midday on November 18th Constable had an express letter from Cadell that almost made him leap from his sickbed with rage, and close on the heels of the courier who brought it came the tremulous figure of Cadell himself. It often irritated Constable to see how easily the fellow got rattled, but this time there was some excuse. He had that morning had a visit from Sir Walter on his way to Court, which was a strange thing, yet not so strange as his visitor's demeanour. For the Sheriff's shaggy brows were drawn and his countenance black as thunder, and there was an unpleasantness in his voice when he requested a private word with Mr. Cadell. After some ominous preliminary hems and an inquiry after Mr. Constable's health he came to the point. He had heard, he said— and from a source that he could not disregard— that Mr. Constable, when he left London, had done so hurriedly, the reason being that his London banker had abruptly stopped his credit and closed his account.[1] Cadell was appalled. He could only assure Sir Walter with the greatest

[1] Lockhart's famous story of how he took the rumour about Constable to Scott at Abbotsford and how Scott, after pooh-poohing it, made an all-night expedition to Polton and back, is picturesque and circumstantial, but cannot be true. Thomas Constable (*Archibald Constable and his Literary Correspondents*) states that he has been unable to find any corroboration in his father's papers, and the contemporary correspondence of Cadell and Constable is conclusive against Lockhart.

earnestness that the story was a malicious fabri-
cation without a word of truth in it. Sir Walter
had said no more, but had hirpled away on his
stick, obviously still perplexed. " An enemy
hath done this," said Constable, and he ordered
his partner to trace the rumour to its source if
possible. That evening—it was a Friday—
Cadell called on Sir Walter in Castle Street, said
he had seen Mr. Constable, who was most
indignant, and would fain know more about the
scandalous story. But Sir Walter's looks had
wonderfully cleared since the morning. He
had only wished, he said, to be in the position
to give a categorical denial to the story, which
had reached him in a letter—from whom he
would not say. Cadell had an inkling that it
was from Lockhart, nor was he far wrong.
Lockhart had repeated the story to Scott on the
authority of a London correspondent. It was
a gross invention; but undoubtedly there were
circumstances to account for it, which circumstances were duly brought home to the writhing
invalid at Polton over the week-end.

The emergency he had always feared but had
never dared to believe possible had arrived.
Hurst & Robinson were tottering. They must
be supported at all costs. He wrote to Cadell
to get into touch with Scott at once with a view
to his joining in a loan of £10,000. Cadell, poor
wretch, was in no case for such a task. He had
spent a hideous week-end making frenzied shifts

to provide for maturing liabilities and had not, as he tearfully protested, had a wink of sleep for thirty-six hours. He would do his best, of course, but even with James Ballantyne's aid he despaired of handling Sir Walter successfully. Would not Constable come up and undertake the business himself; "I think Sir Walter on your representation will do what you propose," he entreated. Next day, "lame as a duck upon his legs, but his heart and courage as firm as a cock," Constable appeared at Castle Street. And Cadell was right. The robust serenity of the man was a convincing argument. Scott agreed to join in supporting the London house. Nothing of consequence happened during the next fortnight. The situation seemed to be easing, and hopeful souls spoke of the worst being over. But in mid-December came a resounding blast that shook the Bank of England itself to its foundations. A big private bank stopped payment, and for several days panic reigned in the City. It was impossible to believe that Hurst & Robinson could escape the general ruin, and on the morning of December 18th James Ballantyne hurried over to Castle Street to tell Scott that the end had come. The more formal news of the failure was to be expected by the next post from London. But in the evening came Cadell. "Ah, how beautiful upon the mountains," quoted Scott when he had gone. For Hurst & Robinson, Cadell

declared, were safe—at least they said they were,
so long as their Scottish friends would stand by
them—and reports from the City generally were
more cheerful. Indeed and indeed the modern
world was strange as any romance ! The author
of *Waverley* had risen that morning a landed
baronet worth £60,000. Before breakfast was
over he had been reduced to beggary, and having
spent the day (spiritually speaking) *in forma
pauperis*, he was now going to bed worth £60,000
once more ! If only he had waited for the
evening post a painful domestic scene would
have been avoided ; for in the interval of beggary
he had been so ill-advised as to break the news
to his wife and had been chidden shrilly for an
egregious fool. Charlotte would hear no ex-
cuses, no explanations. Poor thing, her health
was bad, and asthma does not sweeten the temper,
but still—— That night he wrote in his *Journal* :

" Another person did not afford me all the
sympathy I had expected, perhaps because I did
not need support, yet that is not her nature,
which is generous and kind. She thinks I have
been imprudent, trusting men so far. Perhaps
so—but what could I do ? I must sell my books
to someone, and these folks gave me the largest
price."

If the *Journal* had not been designed for
posthumous publication the entry might have
been fuller and less guarded. For some years
Lady Scott had been in the habit of disguising

her nature by means that her husband did not care to specify.

The Abbotsford Christmas of 1825 was in melancholy contrast to that of 1824. The Lockharts had made their move to London at the beginning of December. Walter was in Ireland with his regiment, and might soon be much farther away, as there was a rumour that the 15th Hussars were about to be ordered to India. Charles, now an Oxford undergraduate, was spending Christmas with the Lockharts. Sir Walter was left alone with Lady Scott and Anne in circumstances that made them depressing companions. Cadell's good tidings had soon lost their first radiance. It was true that Hurst & Robinson had not fallen, but they were still in danger. Constable spoke of going presently to London to assist them by disposing of copyrights. Cadell, again distraught, implored him to lose no time, and Constable retorting angrily that he would use his own judgment, the two fell to quarrelling and recrimination. Scott was bewildered and unhappy, but got some comfort from Constable's robust confidence and unshaken composure. He decided to use his power to borrow £10,000 on the security of Abbotsford. It was the provision he had made for the younger children, but for the common safety it must be risked, and James Ballantyne & Co., loaded with its senior partner's indebtedness, was labouring heavily.

The New Year opened. The Abbotsford mortgage was executed. Reports from London became worse instead of better. It was clear that if Constable were to do anything he must do it at once, yet for some reason he lingered on in Edinburgh, while Cadell entreated, whimpered and sulked. A fortnight passed, and then there came some word that shook even " the Czar's " composure and sent him posthaste to London. Three days later Scott came back to Edinburgh to learn that a bill of Constable's on Hurst & Robinson had been dishonoured. Early next morning a haggard and woebegone James Ballantyne turned up at Castle Street. This time there was no mistake. All three houses were bankrupt. Already arrangements had been made for putting up the shutters of the printing shop. Poor Fatsman ! On trading operations his firm was not only solvent, but in a modest way profitable. The bulk of James Ballantyne's & Co.'s liabilities were due to Scott's reckless borrowings during the fatal period of his sole partnership. Yet in the hour of calamity there was not a word or even a thought of reproach for the man whose infatuated selfishness had brought disaster upon them both. James's mind was still as it had been forty years before in Kelso Grammar School, when the big lame boy from Edinburgh had used to smile across at him and whisper, " Come ower here, Jamie, and I'll tell ye a story." After all, but for Wattie Scott there never would have been a James Ballantyne & Co. Wattie Scott had given and Wattie Scott had taken away. Blessed be the name of Wattie Scott.

Constable returned from London. This last struggle had brought him sensibly nearer death, and it had been in vain. He was beaten, badly beaten ; and in addition he was ill with a malady which renders its victims peculiarly vulnerable to distress, humiliation and anger. Yet, agitated as he was by all these passions, he did not despair. He was still ready to face the world and fight again. By his bankruptcy he had lost all the properties that had made the name of Constable great—he must forfeit the *Encyclopædia Britannica*, the *Waverley* copyrights and his dear child, the *Edinburgh Review*—but he would still have the inchoate *Miscellany*, and, by God, he would be Walter Scott's publisher without any lily-livered Cadell to hamper him.

These things in mind, he repaired without delay to Castle Street, and brave but breathless was ushered into the presence of the Sheriff. His reception was civil enough, but his out-stretched hand was ignored, and before many minutes were past he knew that Scott was done with him. It was not said in so many words. The Sheriff was a courteous gentleman. But the fact that he refused all promise of support was conclusive. At the end of a shattering half-hour the bookseller rose to go. He made a last pathetic effort to break through his host's icy reserve. " Come, come, Sir Walter," he said, " matters may come round, and I trust that you and I may yet crack a cheerful bottle of port together at Abbotsford." He could have said nothing more maladroit. Scott's light blue eyes blazed with anger. " Maister Constable," he replied, " whether we ever meet again under these conditions depends upon circumstances which yet remain to be cleared up." Such was their parting ; and for the first time in his life Constable tasted despair.

Later in the day Scott confided to a friend that the sight of Constable, " puffing like a steamboat," had filled him with loathing. He had made up his mind before the interview— possibly with some assistance from Cadell— that the purple-faced publisher was the villain of the piece ; and now, like the overgrown schoolboy that he was, he could see only offensiveness or absurdity in the man's physical disabilities. His conclusion was not a reasoned one ; he was in no mood for reason. All that concerned him was that the one topic of the day in Parliament Square—and so in all Edinburgh—should be the amazing revelation that Sir Walter Scott, Bt., of Abbotsford, Sheriff of Selkirk, Principal Clerk of the Court of Session, man of letters and friend of princes, had for more than twenty years been a petty tradesman in the Canongate and now could not even pay his debts. Since

Deacon Brodie there had been nothing like it. In the rage of his humiliation Scott's old, long-suppressed antipathy to " the Crafty " revived. To the end of his life he cherished the fixed delusion that it was Constable who had ruined him and brought him to scorn. That he could himself have been the chief contriver of his misfortunes never once occurred to him.

VIII

JAMES BALLANTYNE & Co.'s liabilities in bank-ruptcy amounted to about £120,000, practically all of which was due on bills held by the banks. About one-third of the amount was attributable to the complicated system of mutual support practised by the three houses. The rest was of Scott's own creation. What had happened can be put quite simply. As already stated, Scott between 1816 and 1821 made extravagant pur-chases of land, which he financed by means of bills drawn by James Ballantyne & Co. on Constable & Co. and discounted in the usual way. These bills, amounting to £27,000, were never retired. Constable's credit being good, the banks were always willing to renew, but naturally every renewal meant an addition to the floating debt. Hence Constable's request in 1823 for a substantial reduction, which Scott promised to attend to but did not—on the contrary he went in for fresh borrowings on promissory notes. In the end he paid dearly for his laches. For by way of security for the advances he had given Constable his counter-acceptances for like amounts, and these, when the pinch came, Constable was obliged to put into circulation.

The result was that in the bankruptcy Scott

found himself liable for (*a*) accommodation bills discounted by James Ballantyne & Co. and dishonoured by Constable & Co., £27,000; (*b*) bills to a like amount discounted by Constable & Co. and dishonoured by James Ballantyne & Co.; (*c*) promissory notes, £17,000; and (*d*) discounts, £8,000. In respect of items (*a*) and (*b*), therefore, he was called upon to make good his original borrowings twice over, and there was also a considerable amount of duplicated, or even triplicated, liability in respect of the vicious routine of bill transactions among the three firms. To have to pay the same debt twice is no doubt hard, and it has been usual to express commiseration for Scott on that score. On the other hand, as he had for years taken full advantage of a system of fictitious credit, it was not open to him to complain—nor did he complain—when the same system rendered him liable for a fictitious debt. Further, the importance of the paper inflation of his liabilities must not be exaggerated; for on the most rigorous estimate his net indebtedness was very great— at least £70,000, perhaps over £80,000.

He escaped the shame of the *Gazette*. His creditors, of whom the chief was the Bank of Scotland, were persuaded not to insist upon sequestration, but to accept a private trust of his assets, which consisted of his Edinburgh house and furniture, his life-interest in Abbotsford and a few recent copyrights. There was an agonising

moment when the Bank threatened proceedings
to have the settlement of Abbotsford set aside,
but wiser counsels prevailed, and the Bank
rested content with Scott's binding himself to
be its slave until every penny owing should be
paid. He had many offers of financial assistance,
but refused them all. The pen that had never
yet failed him would not, he was assured, fail
him now. The house in Castle Street and its
furniture were sold. For sixty years the Scotts,
father and son, had been proprietors in Edinburgh
—an old song that deserved a better ending
than a public roup. It was a heart-breaking
business, yet afterwards in his hired lodgings at
Mrs. Brown's, No. 6 St. David Street, when the
voracity of the bugs in his bed and the bickerings
of tipsy Highland chairmen in the street below
kept him awake of nights, Sir Walter forced
himself to count his blessings, viz. that the
roup of his Lares et Penates had fetched £4,000,
or 8d. towards the 20s. in the pound that he had
meant to pay; that he could still afford a beef-
steak and a glass of burgundy for a friend;
and above all that the dear cause of all his
afflictions, Abbotsford, was safe.

To the St. David Street lodgings one evening
in May came word that Charlotte Scott was dead.
She was fifty years of age, or perhaps fifty-one
—it is not certain which, for the exact year as
well as the place of birth is unknown. Her
husband was grieved but quite calm in the face

of an event for which he had long been prepared. For two years she had been visibly a dying woman, and for two months she had been kept miserably alive by doses of digitalis, an unpalatable stimulant. She was buried at Dryburgh a week later. Walter had come from Ireland and Charles had come over from Oxford, but the Lockharts could not leave London, as Sophia had just had a new baby. The widower, attended by his sons, followed the coffin in a coach with undrawn blinds. The deceased having been of the Anglican persuasion, the service was conducted by an excellent young clergyman of the Scottish Episcopal communion, Mr. Ramsay.[1] When all was over Sir Walter faced the assembled company, made a low obeisance and returned to his coach without a word. A week later he was in the old routine of his life in Edinburgh, and beginning a new work of fiction which he had decided to let Cadell have in consideration of his sympathetic behaviour and good counsel during the crisis. His main labour, however, continued to be the *Life of Napoleon*. By the autumn, having used up all his available materials, he was obliged to go to London and Paris for more. In France he found the inns cold and the beds damp. He came home with one more affliction added to his already burdened flesh—chronic rheumatism, which tormented him for the rest of his life.

[1] Dean Ramsay.

Constable bore his fall with simple dignity and unmurmuring fortitude. Stripped of his great possessions, bankrupt in health as well as fortune, betrayed by his partner and deserted by the man he had counted as friend and whose prosperity he had identified with his own, he set himself to the labour of rebuilding the ruined house. The *Miscellany* was after a fashion realised in December 1826, and the reception of the first volumes was encouraging. But he had neither the financial nor the physical resources to carry it to the success of which he had dreamed. Early in the summer of 1827 he put his affairs in order and composed himself for the end. On the afternoon of July 21st, while talking placidly to his eldest son, he collapsed in his arm-chair and died, aged fifty-three. Heaven was merciful. Had he lived a few months longer he would have seen his *Waverley* copyrights put up to auction by his trustee in bankruptcy and knocked down to Cadell and Scott for half of what he had given for them. In the days before the fall he had planned a great new edition of the novels, revised and annotated by the author. Cadell was to do that now.

Least affected by the *débâcle* was James Ballantyne—he was, in fact, hardly affected at all. The trustees in his bankruptcy wisely decided that the printing shop was too good a concern to close down, and carried it on with James as salaried manager under strict business supervision. As the press continued to have contracts for all Scott's printing, it did very well. Ultimately James was able to buy it back, and he ended his days as the proprietor of a flourishing business.

IX

ON April 3rd, 1828, Sir Walter Scott, accompanied by his daughter Anne, set out for London. He had business to attend to, but the chief occasion for the journey was pleasure—some relaxation for himself after two years of anxiety, grief and unremitted toil, and a little gaiety for poor Anne, who was suffering from the effects of filial devotion and the dreariness of Abbotsford. This sorely needed holiday and the temper to enjoy it had been made possible by the excellent state of affairs that Scott's trustees had been able to report to the creditors at the end of 1827. The profits of *Woodstock*, the *Life of Napoleon* and *Chronicles of the Canongate* had been greater than anyone had dared to hope for, while a casual little history book for children, *Tales of a Grandfather*, had proved more popular than any of the novels since *Ivanhoe*. The trust account for the two years had shown a gross income of £40,000, which meant that, whereas in the heyday of his prosperity Scott had never made more than £10,000 or £12,000 a year by his pen, he had been earning since his bankruptcy at the rate of £20,000. A first dividend of six shillings in the pound had convinced the creditors that it would be good policy to encourage so industrious a debtor. It was no longer necessary to

pinch and scheme for paltry sums of ready money.
Some of the old amenities of life had again
become possible—a curious book now and then
(provided it did not cost more than thirty shillings) and, in place of Mrs. Brown's bug-infested
den, a decent furnished house in a good quarter,
fit for Anne to live in.

They travelled south by easy stages, making
a week's journey of it. In London there was
a singularly happy reunion. Walter's regiment
was stationed at Hampton Court. Charles, by
His Majesty's special interest, was now in the
Foreign Office. The Lockharts' little family
had lately been increased to three by the arrival
of baby Charlotte, and they had an elegant new
house in Sussex Place with an outlook over
Regent's Park that put Sir Walter in an ecstasy.
" I have rarely seen," he said, " and could not
have conceived within the precincts of a town
so enchanting a scene as this." For a few days
he was supremely happy, surrounded by his
children and grandchildren, and then Fate
played another spiteful trick.

" I have had hard cards since I came here,"
he wrote to a friend on May 5th. " I had just
had my family here round me, when poor little
Johnny Lockhart was affected with a cough and
fever which threatened and still threatens to
destroy an existence that has always been a frail
one. Lockhart and Sophia instantly removed
the little sufferer to Brighton, where the sea air,

which has always been of service, has something
relieved him. Still the prospect of his attaining
health and strength is greatly diminished, and I
fear almost equal pain to the parents in watching
this frail and flickering light perhaps for a few
years longer, or in seeing it now brought to a
sudden and violent conclusion.

" Anne has thrown up her invitations, tickets
to Almack's and all the amusements which her
friends were providing for her to attend to
Sophia in her distress. So here I am, melancholy
enough, and some law matters are like to keep
me till the 20th of the month, when I hope we
will meet in Edinburgh." [1]

Notwithstanding his melancholy Sir Walter
found London so tolerable that he prolonged his
stay by a week, and when he turned homewards
he reckoned that the trip had been well worth
the time and money. A rather exacting round
of social enjoyments had proved to him that he
stood as well as ever with the best people.
Item, he had had another snug little dinner with
the King. *Item*, he had dined with the Duchess
of Kent and been presented to the Princess
Victoria, a plain-looking child of nine, whose
absurd name he trusted would be changed when
she came to the Throne. *Item*, he had heard a
great deal of gossip. *Item*, he had pulled some
political strings on Lockhart's behalf and cadged
jobs for the sons of certain friends. *Item*, he
had sat for Chantrey, Haydon and Northcote.

[1] See note at end.

Item, he had successfully opposed a private bill that appeared to threaten the amenity of Abbotsford. *Item*, he had had a good rest and felt nearly, if not quite, as fit as a Hercules for the new labours that awaited him.

At home he found nothing but good news. Worthy Mr. Cadell was in great spirits. *The Fair Maid of Perth*, which had been published at the end of April, was doing uncommonly well. Scott wrote in his *Journal* : " A disappointment being always to be apprehended, I too am greatly pleased that the evil day is adjourned, for the time must come—and yet I can spin a tough yarn still with anyone now going." God willing, he would spin a few more—he had engaged with Cadell for three—before he was finished. Better still, his trustees, after much heart-searching, were disposed to finance Cadell's great scheme for a uniform edition of the Waverley Novels, revised and annotated by the author. This, the *Magnum Opus*, as Scott called it, would appear under the author's name. For the great *Waverley* mystification was over, brought like other pleasant things to a rude end by the events of 1826.[1] The investigation of Constable's affairs in course of law had revealed everything. No matter : the jest had long gone stale, and

[1] The so-called disclosure by Lord Meadowbank at the Theatrical Fund dinner of February 23rd, 1827, was not in any real sense a disclosure, but only a formal compliment to Scott on the occasion of his first public appearance since his misfortunes. Scott himself attached little importance to it.

the *Magnum* would be all the better for being the acknowledged work of Sir Walter Scott, Bt. So, buckling to his task again, Sir Walter Scott, Bt., began writing new introductions full of curious information, and what he could not get into the introductions he embodied in a formidable apparatus of notes, historical and anecdotal. He also wrote another novel, *Anne of Geierstein*, more *Tales of a Grandfather* and a History of Scotland for Lardner's *Cyclopædia*. Boldest, most persevering of all baronets, he wrote early in the morning and late into the night. He stinted himself of rest and of amusement. He very much wanted to see the celebrated Mr. Burke of the West Port hanged, and bespoke a window for the occasion, yet at the last moment found he could not afford the time even for so simple and edifying a pleasure. The *Journal* was neglected. When after six months he braced himself to resume it he wrote quite truthfully :

"During this period nothing has happened worth particular notice. The same occupations, the same amusements, the same occasional alternations of spirits, gay or depressed, the same absence of all sensible or rational cause for the one or the other. I half grieve to take up my pen and doubt if it is worth while to record such an infinite quantity of nothing . . . I cannot say I have been happy, for the feeling of increasing weakness in my lame leg is a great affliction. I walk now with pain and difficulty at all times, and it sinks my soul to think how soon I may be altogether a disabled cripple. I am tedious to my friends, and I doubt the sense of it makes me fretful. Everything else goes well enough. My cash affairs are clearing, and though last year was an expensive one, I have been paying debt. Yet I have a dull contest before me which will probably outlast my life."

He had, in fact, turned himself into a writing machine concerning which the only question was how long it would last and how much could be got out of it before it broke down. For nearly a year it functioned magnificently. But one day in the early summer of 1829 Scott had to go to bed and send in haste for his doctor. He was bleeding profusely from the bowels. Dr. Ross, an excellent practitioner of the Sangrado school, treated him *secundum artem*—that is, cupped and bled and starved him and reduced his daily allowance of strong drink to a thing *pour rire*. The best advice would have been to stop work, but if given, it was not taken. The patient recovered and resumed the whole of his labours and some of his liberality in eating and drinking. But he was increasingly sensible of fatigue now, was apt to fall asleep at his desk, and could not take a walk at Abbotsford without the supporting arm of Tom Purdie, the surly ex-poacher who had been his personal attendant and factotum for thirty years. It was Tom's humour to die suddenly towards the end of that year. He was an ill-conditioned dog, but faithful, and his master lamented him if no one else did. A successor of sorts was found, whose duties were to prove more exacting than ever old Tom's had been, for within three months he had to take charge of a difficult paralytic. On the afternoon of February 15th, 1830, shortly after getting home from Court, Sir Walter fell down in an apoplectic fit.

Life, with its abundance of tragic materials, is careless of tragic forms. The four years' magnificent conflict with adversity deserved at the least a clean and decent end, and death could never have come to Scott more fittingly than in the spring of 1830, when he knew that his task was virtually accomplished and that, whether he lived or died, his creditors would in time be paid to the uttermost farthing. But no such appropriate grace was given him. The stroke was not mortal. Drs. Ross and Abercrombie were at hand with their bleedings and cuppings and starvings to preserve for two and a half years a mere existence that was yet interwoven with lively and various sufferings—a salvage unsightly and most pitiable. At first it seemed not very bad. There was a specious recovery. In a week or two the patient reappeared in Parliament House, genial as ever and not appreciably altered, save for a new twist in the smiling mouth and an unaccustomed stammer when in reply to inquiries about his illness he explained that his stomach had been giving him trouble—a foolish placebo of the doctors that he did his best to believe. But presently headquarters began to hint that his retirement on pension would facilitate a reorganisation of the clerical staff of the Court of Session. Subject to some heart-searchings—mainly as to the proportion of his salary the Treasury would agree for pension—he accepted his dismissal calmly enough. It meant so much more time for writing—more notes for the *Magnum*, more romances, more histories, more curious and voluminous odds and ends for the reviews. Hitherto his writing had been a means to an end ; now it was a sick man's obsession.

The copy was produced as punctually as ever and even more abundantly ; but publisher and printer took to glancing at each other in alarm, and soon dreaded the arrival of each succeeding parcel from Abbotsford with its unconscious instalment of the new tale of physical and mental decay. To appeal to Scott to stop work for his health's sake was useless. Already his doctors had warned him and received churlish answers. To a remonstrance from the favoured Lockhart he was more amiable but not less obstinate. " I understand you, and thank you from my heart," he said, " but I must tell you at once how it is with me. I am not sure that I am quite myself in all things ; but I am sure that in one point there is no change. I mean that I foresee distinctly that if I were to be idle I should go mad. In comparison to this, death is no risk to shrink from." And so it went on. It vexed him, as he covered sheet after sheet, that the mere mechanism of writing should have become so difficult. His fingers played unaccountable pranks with the pen and suffered cruelly from chilblains when the weather turned cold, but, anyhow, he felt his mind as clear as ever. So much so that he was very insistent upon its clearness.

One day towards the end of the year Cadell and Ballantyne met in agitated conference. The opening chapters of a new novel, *Count Robert of Paris*, had come to hand, and they were shocking. James, who since the death of Will Erskine was the only man who possessed the license to criticise the master's work, was deputed to explain in writing that the subject of the novel was unsuitable and that not even the genius of the author of *Waverley* could make the Byzantine Court interesting to the British public. A tart reply came back from Abbotsford :

" If I were like other authors, which I flatter myself I am not, I should send you an order on my treasurer for a hundred ducats, wishing you all prosperity and a little more taste ; but having never supposed that any abilities I ever had were of a perpetual texture, I am glad when friends tell me what I might be long in finding out myself. Mr. Cadell will show you what I have written to him. My present idea is to go abroad for a few months, if I hold together as long. So ended the Fathers of the Novel—Fielding and Smollett—and it would be no unprofessional finish for yours,—Walter Scott."

The letter to Cadell was a jumble of obstinacy, vacillation and wounded pride. No doubt his day was done and he ought to retire—not because he was failing, but because there was so much competition nowadays. "The fact is, I have not only written a great deal myself, but, as Bobadil teaches his companions to fence, I have taught a hundred gentlemen to write nearly as well, if not altogether so, as myself." He could not admit that *Count Robert* was a bad book, so for the present let the printing proceed.

Cadell and Ballantyne were dismayed. This quavering arrogance raised a question that would hardly bear thinking about—Would they be driven to tell Scott that he must either stop or be stopped? While they paused the post brought Cadell another letter. The stricken man's mood had changed. Here were no more reproaches, only a piteous appeal for friendly consideration and counsel, for he had to confess something that he had kept from them, viz. that lately he had had a second stroke.

" Now in the midst of all this, I began my work with as much attention as I could ; and having taken pains with my story, I find it is not relished, nor indeed tolerated by those who have

no interest in condemning it, but a strong interest
in putting even a face upon their consciences.
Was not this, in the circumstances, a damper to
an invalid, already afraid that the sharp edge
might be taken off his intellect, though he was
not himself sensible of that ? and did it not seem
of course, that nature was rather calling for
repose than for further efforts in a very excitable
and feverish style of composition ? It would
have been the height of injustice and cruelty to
impute want of friendship or sympathy to J. B.'s
discharge of a doubtful and, I am sensible, a
perilous task. . . . It is the consciousness of
his sincerity which makes me doubt whether I
can proceed with the County Paris. I am most
anxious to do justice to all concerned, and yet
for the soul of me, I cannot see what is likely to
turn out for the best. I might attempt the
Perilous Castle of Douglas, but I fear the subject
is too much used, and that I might again fail in
it. Then being idle will never do, for a thousand
reasons. All this I am thinking of till I am half
sick. I wish James, who gives such stout
advice when he thinks we are wrong, would tell
us how to put things right. One is tempted to
cry ' Wo worth thee ! is there no help in thee ? '
Perhaps it may be better to take no resolution
till we all meet together."

The very pain and reason of this letter, witness-
ing as it did that whatever had happened to the
novelist the correspondent was able to collect
himself, made the problem worse. Before it
could be answered came this intimation : having
been obliged to lay *Count Robert* aside, yet being

incapable of idleness, Sir Walter had composed
a very serious pamphlet on the great political
question of the moment, wherein was shown
by many clear and abundant proofs—that is,
to anyone who was not a Whig or a blackguard
—the absurdity as well as the infamy of Lord
Grey's proposals for Parliamentary reform.
It was intended for immediate publication.
Sir Walter was sure it would make a profound
impression on the public.

Cadell and Ballantyne shared his certainty—
so much so that they hastened down to Abbotsford, quaking in concert but resolved that at all
costs this madness must be stopped. They were
given pause by their reception. Sir Walter,
looking fairly well, greeted them with perfect
composure and affability. He was eager to
discuss the good news he had just had from
Edinburgh—how his creditors had received a
second large dividend, and how generously they
had shown their appreciation of his efforts by
releasing from the trust assets his plate, library
and collection of curios and armour. His
mind was easy now, he said, and he could make
his will in the knowledge that, thanks to the
Magnum Opus, the rest of the debt would be
wiped out in a few years, even if he never wrote
another line. So seriously and sensibly did he
talk that evening that Cadell and Ballantyne
went to bed greatly relieved.

The morning brought a different story. Im-

mediately after breakfast the great pamphlet was
produced, and until noon the two men had to
sit in patient misery while their host droned
and stammered and drivelled through interminable periods of stale argument, labouring rhetoric
and unhappy invective. Cadell, trying to combine tact with emphasis, asked if Sir Walter had
realised the consequences of such a publication.
Sir Walter, calling his bushy eyebrows into
play, replied that the consequences might be
damned. Cadell rejoined that they certainly
would, and the *Magnum Opus* would be damned
into the bargain if the author appeared in the
character of an anti-Reform pamphleteer. Sir
Walter, never having thought of that, looked
blank and appealed to James. Poor James
tremulously ventured to homologate *in toto*. A
painful half-hour ensued. It ended in an awkward compromise. James had for many years
issued from his press a little Tory newspaper,
which called itself by the name of the *Weekly
Journal*, and it was agreed that, subject to some
modification and the very strictest anonymity,
Sir Walter's diatribe might appear in its columns
without doing any harm to anybody. It never
did appear. When James sent the proofs he
had so many alterations to suggest that Scott
in a pet flung the whole wretched thing upon
his study fire.

But if he might not use his pen he could still
raise his voice against the abomination of deso-

lation. As Sheriff of Selkirk he was returning officer for the county, a situation which, according to the public morality of the day, was regarded as an opportunity rather than a disqualification for party activity, and it was certainly no part of Scott's political creed to be in advance of his time. Crippled, palsied, dying, he could see himself as the Tyrtæus of the Border Tories. The Border Tories saw otherwise, and snubbed Tyrtæus so cruelly that he was in half a mind to quit the field. Yet no—his neighbours might be poor rats, but he at least would do his duty. " I will make my opinion public at every place where I shall be called upon or expected to appear," he wrote in his *Journal*, " but I will not thrust myself forward again. May the Lord have mercy upon us and incline our hearts to keep this vow ! " His prayer was not answered, for within ten days of writing these words he announced his intention of moving an anti-Reform resolution at a meeting of the Roxburgh freeholders at Jedburgh. Anne, weeping bitterly, implored him not to go. Her solicitude was rewarded with one of the terrible outbursts of fury that for the past year had made Abbotsford an ill place to live in. Sir Walter went to Jedburgh to face, not a decent gathering of county freeholders, but a mob of Reform townsfolk who were in no mood to endure a long rambling mumbled discourse, of which they could hear little and that not to their liking. They howled him down. When the meeting ended he bowed gravely to the jeering artisans and pronounced with as much audibility and scorn as his trembling lips could compass, the words " Moriturus vos saluto."

The dying gladiator had one more blow to strike. On April 23rd, the Reform Bill having been wrecked in the Commons, Lord Grey appealed with confidence to an infuriated country. When the crisis came Scott was lying speechless at Abbotsford in a third attack of apoplexy so grave that Walter and the Lockharts hastened to his bedside hardly daring to hope that they would see him alive. Yet once more he rallied, got something like speech back, contrived after a fashion to attend to his duties as returning officer for Selkirk, and even resumed writing a little. A less satisfactory feature of his sense of recovery was his avowed purpose of going to Jedburgh on election day to cast his last vote and make his last speech. The protests of his family were eagerly seconded by his political friends, including the Tory candidate himself, who assured him that his assistance was not needed, yet dared not say what was the fact, that it was not wanted. With the cunning of a clouded mind Scott pretended to be persuaded, but secretly gave orders for his carriage to be ready early on the morning of the poll. When he reached Jedburgh the town was in an uproar. The local rabble, reinforced by a horde of weavers from Hawick, were parading the streets with drums and banners and demonstrating the virtue of democracy by maltreating anyone who did not sport the Whig colours. They pelted Scott's carriage with stones, howled, cursed and spat at him as he hobbled slowly to the Court-house, supported by two friends. When all was over and the Tory had been returned by the handsome majority of forty votes to nineteen, a kindly Whig smuggled him through a back lane to his carriage. The mob, inflamed by defeat and an arduous day's drinking, pursued him out of the burgh with yells of " Burke Sir Walter ! " and sped him homeward over the bridge with a parting shower of brickbats. " Sad blackguards," he wrote in his *Journal* that evening ; " Troja fuit."

The times were out of joint—that was certain. Nobody could be trusted, not even James Ballantyne. Two years before James had had the misfortune to lose his wife, and had never been the same man since. Scott, speaking with the authority of one who was himself a widower, had exhorted him to fortitude in affliction, but James, who had loved his wife, would not be comforted. He became excessively devout, an extravagance which Scott might have forgiven if the new-found faith in God had not been accompanied by a loss of faith in the Tory party. During the summer the *Weekly Journal* announced James's definite adherence to Reform. Scott

156

passionately vowed that never more should
James Ballantyne be his literary adviser—a
punishment that the poor printer accepted
philosophically, for it relieved him of the painful duty of saying what he thought of *Castle
Dangerous*. The appearance of friendship was
kept up, however, and one Saturday in July
James went down to Abbotsford for the week-
end. It was not a fortunate visit. Scott could
not keep off politics and broke out in railing
accusations against his oldest friend, who could
only reply, " The Lord rebuke thee." Early
next morning, without waiting to see his host,
James departed. He left word that his spiritual
health demanded more strenuous devotional
exercises on the Sabbath Day than Abbotsford
afforded, on hearing which Sir Walter swore a
little. They never met again.

On November 1st, 1831, owing to persistent
head winds, H.M. frigate *Barham*, of fifty guns,
Captain Pigot, bound for Malta and Naples and
three days out from Portsmouth, was still beating
up and down in sight of Land's End. She
carried as passengers the celebrated Sir Walter
Scott, Bt., Major Walter Scott, of the 15th Hussars,
Mrs. Scott and Miss Scott, who were all very
sea-sick, though the old gentleman was wonderfully determined about appearing on deck and
taking as much fresh air and exercise as his
infirmities would allow. These infirmities were

many. He could not walk without support and had some queer surgical apparatus fitted to his right leg that clanked and creaked. He liked to amuse the officers with droll stories, but his speech, even allowing for a Scotch accent, was not very clear, and he was apt to tell the same droll story twice within five minutes. He sometimes said that it was a great pity His Majesty's ships were not propelled by steam, which suggested that his intellects were slightly deranged.

The Bay of Biscay in the month of November holds little pleasure for an elderly invalid, and it cannot be said that Scott enjoyed his journey to the Mediterranean. But he was deeply gratified by the generosity of the Whig Ministers who had arranged it—it was evident, he said, that in spite of Reform things were still in the hands of gentlemen—and the novelty of everything kept his mind occupied. On reaching Malta he decided that his next novel should deal with the island of St. Paul and the Knights Hospitallers. The *Barham* took him on to Naples in time to spend Christmas with his younger son, who was attached to the British Legation. He stayed there for four months, a little confused and impatient about things, but not unhappy. In the mornings he worked diligently at the *Siege of Malta* and a shorter tale called *Il Bizarro*, which he thought well of, but are still in manuscript. He found it amusing to collect Neapoli-

tan ballads and study the dialect. He went to
see Pompeii and other sights, put on his Royal
Archer's uniform to attend a levee of his Sicilian
Majesty, and dined out more freely and often
than was good for him. There were moments
when he comprehended everything and became
depressed, but ordinarily he lived in a state of
vague elation and blunted sensibility which
protected him from all the shocks of reality, even
the death of the beloved little Johnny Lockhart.
He began to dream that he was out of debt and
rich again and even getting well.

"My story of Malta," he wrote to Lockhart,
"will be with you by the time you have finished
the Letters; and if it succeeds it will in a great
measure enable me to attain the long projected
and very desirable object of clearing me from
all old encumbrances and expiring as rich a man
as I could desire in my own freehold. And
when you recollect that this has been wrought
out in six years, the sum amounting to at least
£120,000, it is somewhat of a novelty in literature.
I shall be as happy and rich as I please for the
last days of my life and play the good papa with
my family without thinking on pounds, shillings
and pence. . . . After the *Siege of Malta* I intend
to close [the series] of *Waverley* with a poem in
the style of the *Lay*, or rather of the *Lady of the
Lake*, to be a L'Envoy, or final postscript to
these tales. The subject is a curious tale of
chivalry belonging to Rhodes. Sir Frederick
Adam will give me a cast of a steam-boat to
visit Greece, and you will come and go with

me. . . . We will return to Europe through Germany and see what peradventure we shall behold."

The unexpected transfer of Sir Frederick Adam from the Ionian Islands to India having put an end to the Greek project, Scott's interest in foreign travel, such as it was, disappeared. All he wanted now was to visit Goethe at Weimar and get home as soon as possible; and when at the end of March he heard that Goethe was dead, the crazy façade that was all that remained of his spirit crumbled into ruin. He became morose and intractable, iterating daily his one desire, " Let us to Abbotsford." Charles accompanied him to Rome, where he spent three apathetic weeks, and on May 11th the homeward journey was begun. The party travelled via Venice, Innsbruck, Ulm, Frankfort and Cologne. On June 9th near Nimeguen the sick man had a fourth stroke of apoplexy which left him completely paralysed. On July 11th he reached Abbotsford. The beloved walls and his native air seemed to revive him somewhat, for the end did not come until September 21st.

So died, in his sixty-second year, Walter Scott, the simplest, sincerest and greatest of all romantics. To others romanticism might afford a metaphysic or an artistic theory or a gesture; to him it was a religion, a creed to be accepted and a life to be lived. But the romantic life is not a practical proposition : indeed, like raising oneself by the hair of the head, it is a contradiction in terms, for the essence of romance is that the life it reveals was never lived on sea or land. Scott never understood that. He never really understood anything, for though he had solid reasoning powers, he had little insight. He lived in terms of feeling and believing and willing, and spent his days pursuing incompatibles with unremitting diligence and spectacular, if sometimes sad, results. He was a professional man who aspired to be a feudal lord and could not keep his fingers out of trade ; a Jacobite whose devotion to the House of Hanover became a byword ; an enthusiastic admirer of the material progress of his age who would not accept its social and political consequences ; an Anglophobe in principle who in practice found England altogether admirable ; an historian who knew everything about history except its meaning. To a moderately clever man these absurdities would have been obvious, but Scott was not even moderately clever. Of the metaphysical diathesis that is said to distinguish his countrymen he had not a trace. He loved to talk, but was never at ease in a discussion and never said anything worth remembering. His writings are as bare of ideas as his conversation was.

But if he conspicuously lacked the higher intellectual qualities, he had the endowment most suited to express his genius—an inexhaustible invention, a formidable memory, a sharp, though superficial eye for character, a gusto for the human pageant and a power of application that enabled him in ten years to produce more than Dickens produced in twenty. To discuss the quality of his genius is no part of the present study, and merely to extol its magnificence would be an idle and impertinent display of brave words. It is enough to say that in the history of prose fiction there are but two epoch-makers—Cervantes, who did the ancient and beloved art of pure story-telling to a cruel death, and Walter Scott, who brought it to a glorious resurrection.

.　　.　　.　　.　　.

With the death of James Ballantyne, four months after his friend and patron, the last of the oddly assorted *Waverley* syndicate vanished into the common earth. And now, the Court of Denmark being all dead, what of Fortinbras, to wit, Robert Cadell ?

> " For me, with sorrow I embrace my fortune :
> I have some rights of memory in this kingdom,
> Which now to claim my vantage doth invite me."

After Scott's death Mr. Cadell very kindly undertook to pay off some £30,000 of liabilities still outstanding in consideration of an assignment of the future profits of Scott's copyrights. He had already done very well out of the Waverley Novels and continued so to do. Fifteen years

later, on the lamented death without issue of
Colonel Sir Walter Scott, second and last baronet,
he took the opportunity of approaching Lockhart, whose two minor children were now the
only surviving descendants of the great Sir
Walter. He proposed a final settlement. According to his books he had not yet been re-
couped, but that was only a question of time and
he made no point of it. What he now suggested
was that he should relieve the family of the
mortgage of £10,000 on Abbotsford which had
been executed in the crisis of 1825. In return
he asked no more than the assignment of the
remaining rights in Scott's work, the future
profits of Lockhart's *Life of Scott* and the preparation *gratis* by Lockhart of an abridgment
of the *Life* suitable for popular publication.
Lockhart made a wry face, but agreed. Mr.
Cadell died two years later very rich. He was
a clever man in his day, but is not now greatly
remembered.

[The letter quoted on page 142 and now published for the first time was written to Lord Chief
Commissioner Adam. The full text is as follows.

My dear Lord Commissioner,
    I find you have been led into a natural
mistake by a letter from Reynolds, the editor of
the Keepsake.
    I suppose some change has taken place in the

destination of your picture. He ought to have informed you that he is an only (*sic*) literary editor of the work, a supercargo who looks after matters in general, with a salary I suppose for so doing. Heath is proprietor of the work, and it is to him and not to Reynolds, that the picture with your permission, will be entrusted, and who has written me last week a letter making himself responsible for its safe *return* against the first of September, i.e. if it is presently put into his hands. He is a very wealthy and respectable man and now pleads illness for having kept the picture too long when it was the Duke of Bedford's. I hope this will explain the confusion, and that Maida will have this additional chance of celebrity.

I have had hard cards since I came here. I had just seen my family here round me when poor little Johnny Lockhart was affected with a cough and fever which threatened and still threatens to destroy an existence which has always been a frail one. Lockhart and Sophia instantly removed with the little sufferer to Brighton, where the sea air, which had always been of service, has something relieved him. Still the prospect of his attaining health and strength is greatly diminished, and I fear almost equal pain to the parents in watching this frail and flickering light perhaps for a few years longer or in seeing it now brought to a sudden and violent conclusion.

Anne has thrown up her invitations, tickets to Almack's which her friends were providing for her to attend to Sophia in her distress. So here I am, melancholy enough, and some law matters are like to keep me till the 20th of this month, when I hope we will meet in Edinburgh. I have seen Mr. Locker and Mr. Charles Adam. I hear of the latter's prospects from every quarter.

My kindest respects to Miss Louisa Adam, and I allways am with the utmost respect and affection.

Your Lordship's truly obliged,

WALTER SCOTT.

24 SUSSEX PLACE,
REGENT PARK,
5 *May.*

I have rarely seen, and could not have conceived within the precincts of a town, so enchanting a scene as this.]

THE ETTRICK SHEPHERD

I

Washington Irving records that when he went to Abbotsford in August 1817 he found the hospitality more admirable than the scenery. Scott took him for a ramble in the hills and demonstrated the landscape with his walking-stick, rolling off his tongue with evident emotion all the lovely names—Lammermuir and Smailholm, Torwoodlee and Gala Water, Teviotdale, Yarrow and Ettrick. Irving hardly knew what to say.

"I gazed about me for a time with mute surprise, I may almost say, with disappointment. I beheld a mere succession of grey waving hills, line beyond line, as far as my eye could reach, monotonous in their aspect, and so destitute of trees that one could almost see a stout fly walking along their profile; and the far-famed Tweed appeared a naked stream, flowing between bare hills, without a tree or thicket on its banks."

He murmured something complimentary about the genius that could extract romance from the most unpromising materials. Scott was vexed. Among his neighbours he enjoyed the title of " King of the Forest," and his domains were dear to him. Granted that " the Forest " was no forest but a tumbled treeless desert—

JAMES HOGG
From a drawing by D. Maclise, R.A.

" lucus a non lucendo "—there was more in it
than could meet the eye of any Yankee, however
kindly.

The fact remained that the great bulk of the
" King of the Forest's " subjects were sheep and
that in most parts of Selkirkshire human beings
were as scarce as trees. To-day the population
of the county is something under 25,000. A
hundred years ago it was considerably less.
Then, as now, three-fourths of the population
were concentrated in the east corner, where the
Ettrick and the Gala join the Tweed—that is,
in the immediate neighbourhood of Abbotsford.
It was there that the wool from the landward
districts was turned into cloth. Tweedside was
well enough, and if you turned up the Ettrick
Water you would be within the pale of civilisation
as far as the burgh of Selkirk. But after Selkirk
you entered the wilds and at the hamlet of
Ettrick Kirk, far up the vale, you came to the
ultimate degree of remoteness and solitude.
The scattered inhabitants of this desolate region
were sheep-farmers and their shepherds. Compared with the farmers and weavers of Tweedside, they were an uncouth illiterate folk, who
in dress and manners had changed little since
the seventeenth century, but they had the
shepherd's saving grace of occasional mobility.
The tiller of the soil and the craftsman are bound
to their parish, but the shepherd must come
down from his hills and travel to distant markets,

north, south, east and west, to buy and sell his
sheep. The shepherds of Ettrick were rough
but travelled men. They knew no frontiers.
They drove their sheep across the Borders to
Wooler in the east and Carlisle in the south, and
across the Highland line to Strathearn and
Tayside and even farther. They were Arcadians
and proud of it, but they knew their ways about
the world and could hold their own in Edinburgh or Glasgow—or London, for that matter,
for sometimes they went very far south.

When at the end of 1799 Scott became Sheriff
of Selkirk his acquaintance with these people
was comparatively slight. He had childish
memories of his grandfather's shepherds at
Sandyknowe, but Sandyknowe is in the north-
eastern extremity of the Forest, and as for the
Border holidays of his later boyhood, they had
been spent under the eye of a maiden aunt at
Kelso, which is still farther east and not in the
Forest at all. It was not until his expeditions
in search of materials for the *Border Minstrelsy*
that his knowledge of the life of the uplands
really began. Even after his appointment as
Sheriff he continued for some time to live at
Lasswade, and came to the Forest only as a
visitor, though necessarily a frequent one.

He was often accompanied on his excursions
by a wild-looking familiar spirit—young John
Leyden, poor student, poet and orientalist, who
was his principal assistant, or rather collaborator,

in the *Border Minstrelsy*. This unkempt and
hungry genius had been discovered in Constable's
shop by Richard Heber, who lost no time in
introducing him to Scott, and Scott had every
reason to bless the lucky chance that brought
them together. Leyden's learning—especially
in linguistics—was immense, and it was the
learning of a disciplined scholar, very different
from the fascinating but disorderly collection of
oddments that filled the chambers of Scott's
brain. When the plan for a modest little volume
of Border ballads was explained to him he snorted
contemptuously and immediately took charge
of the situation. Himself a shepherd's son from
a remote corner of Roxburgh, he knew that the
amount of oral tradition available was far greater
than Scott imagined, and he also knew how to
come at it. Under his influence the limited and
amateurish plan that Scott had been content with
was discarded, and the *Border Minstrelsy* was
carried out as a serious and substantial work of
scholarship.

The *Minstrelsy* contains a certain number of
spurious ballads, and had it not been for Leyden
would probably have contained many more.
In antiquarian matters Scott was as gullible as
any Monkbarns or Pickwick, but Leyden's eye
was sharp and suspicious and looked askance
at any ballad as to which particulars of prove-
nance and antecedents were lacking or scanty.
For example, he had doubts about some pieces

that came to hand from a Yarrow correspondent, named William Laidlaw. Neither Scott nor Leyden had ever met Mr. Laidlaw. They had been put into touch with him by a Selkirk man, now resident in Edinburgh, from whom they learned that he was the son of a prosperous sheep-farmer and, being of a literary turn, was eager to assist them in their work. The pieces he sent from time to time were undoubtedly interesting ; but he gave no account of them save that he had had them from one James Hogg, a shepherd who had for a good many years been in his father's employ and was known locally as " Jamie the Poeter." The fact that this Hogg was some sort of a bard himself was a little suspicious. Accordingly the poems were not included in the first two volumes of the *Minstrelsy*, but were held over until Scott and Leyden should have an opportunity of seeing Mr. Laidlaw.

The two volumes were published in January 1802. One day, during the spring vacation following, Scott and Leyden rode out to the farm of Blackhouse in Yarrow. Will Laidlaw proved to be a youth of twenty-two or twenty-three, of an ingenuous and enthusiastic disposition to whom Scott's heart warmed at once. The meeting was the beginning of a lifelong friendship. Later, in the days of Abbotsford's glory, Will Laidlaw—though he was nearly as unbusinesslike as the Ballantynes and had been a sad failure as a farmer on his own account—

was installed as the Sheriff's steward; and when the evil days came he was the faithful amanuensis who bore with all his stricken patron's humours and at the end was the dying man's sick-nurse and companion.

Will had a new treasure to show—the ballad of " Auld Maitland and his three Sons "—which was of a quality that left nothing to be desired. Even Leyden's habitual doubts were for the moment consumed in the fire of his enthusiasm. But presently they arose from their ashes with redoubled strength. Will's story was that he had taken down " Auld Maitland " from the mouth of one of the Blackhouse servant girls, who in turn alleged that she had learned it from Jamie the Poeter's old mother. Here was the Poeter again. Every path seemed to lead back to him. Leyden interrogated Will sharply. Did not " this Hogg " write verses himself? Oh, yes, and very fine verses too. He had even had some of them printed in a book, which unfortunately nobody would buy.

" I trust," growled Leyden, " there is no fear of his passing off any of his own verses on Mr. Scott for old ballads?"

Will Laidlaw hastened to protest Jamie's strict honesty. Leyden was not appeased.

" Let him beware of forgery," he roared with a ferocity that set poor Will quaking. " Let him beware of forgery! "

The more the collectors studied " Auld Maitland " the more they admired it and the less they were disposed to accept it as genuine without further inquiry. A few weeks later they were back at Blackhouse demanding to see " this Hogg " face to face. Will Laidlaw took them to his cousin's farm at Ramsaycleugh up the Vale of Ettrick. There a messenger was sent out to find Jamie Hogg, and in half an hour or so a very singular being was introduced. He was a young man of Scott's own age, of goodish stature, strong and graceful, his face handsome, with short clear-cut features, fair complexion and light blue eyes, and when he doffed his bonnet a mighty cataract of light red hair flooded his back and shoulders. He wore the traditional dress of his district and calling—a maud or chequered plaid, short blue jacket and gamashes. His speech was rough but ready, and his whole bearing showed a marked, even alarming, freedom from constraint. He expressed himself as highly honoured by the presence of two such distinguished persons as Mr. Scott and Mr. Leyden, but he also made it clear that he was not to be intimidated either by the official dignity of the one or the college erudition of the other. He brought with him a bundle of ballads in manuscript, including " Auld Maitland," as to which he assured the gentlemen that if they still doubted they would be welcome at his cottage at Ettrickhouse, where they would hear the ballad from the lips of his old mother. Nothing could be fairer. The invitation having been accepted for the following day, the company settled down to a social evening. " The Sheriff told his queerest stories ; the Shepherd's laugh was ready chorus." Years afterwards the Shepherd's appreciation of the Sheriff's anecdotage was somewhat diminished, for, truth to tell, its characteristic was profusion rather than point.[1]

The visit to the Hogg household next morning was on the whole a success. In honour of the occasion Jamie had somehow procured a bottle of fiery claret, which he proposed the Sheriff should empty with him. He was a thought vexed when the Sheriff, after a single glass, made the excuse that a man in his position had to be very careful, but he took speedy comfort in the reflection that the less the guest took the more there was left for the host. As for old Mrs. Hogg, she turned out to be even more alarming than her son. Her candour was formidable. Before she would recite " Auld Maitland," she must needs tell the Sheriff that she had read his book and found it deplorable from every point

---

[1] Hogg in *The Domestic Manners of Sir Walter Scott* says he never heard Scott tell the same story twice, but allowance must be made for obituary piety. In *Noctes Ambrosianæ* he is made to speak very contemptuously of Scott's stories—" nine out o' ten o' them meaning naething, and the tenth as auld as the Eildon Hills." In drawing his picture of the Shepherd, " Christopher North " admittedly gave liberal play to his invention, but he would hardly have dared to invent that. Hogg must have said something of the kind ; and the fact that Wilson preserved it confirms the suspicion which creeps into one's mind even from Lockhart's pages—that Sir Walter in his anecdotal vein was apt to be a bore.

of view. His versions were corrupt, he could not spell, and in any case his idea of a book of ballads was a contradiction in terms, for it was of the essence of a ballad that it should be recited or sung, and to reduce it to the mechanical terms of print was to destroy its soul. Scott humbly agreed that this might be so. Then Jamie had his say. He could not agree with his mother's strictures. There was nothing wrong with the Sheriff's versions of the old ballads. On the other hand, he was bound to confess that he had been disappointed, deeply disappointed, in the imitations—in fact, he was inclined to think that he could do better himself.

At this the Sheriff smiled and Leyden looked up sharply. It happened to be true. The Ettrick Shepherd had the finest natural gift of literary imitation of any man then living. Scott's sham antiques have their own charm, but as a representation of the ancient manner Hogg's *Kilmeny* is far better than anything Scott ever wrote. Scott laughed heartily at the parody of himself in *Rejected Addresses*, but when Hogg did the same thing—only better—in *The Poetic Mirror* he regarded it as a tasteless liberty. From their first meeting to the end of his life Scott's attitude to Hogg never materially changed. As Robert Burns was to him the "high-souled plebeian" to be distantly admired but never visited, so Hogg was the highly talented rustic who deserved encouragement of his superiors in the world, but who must be kept in his place. Hogg, who, unlike Burns, was a very simple egoist, never seems to have been aware of this canon. He had an assured, but, as events showed, by no means an exaggerated opinion of his abilities, and it never occurred to him that, as between two men of letters, Jamie Hogg should lower his flag to Wattie Scot merely because Wattie Scott was a sheriff and Jamie Hogg was a shepherd. The stony social wall against which Burns so often and so bloodily battered his proud head simply did not exist for his brother of Ettrick ; and what the one preached defiantly in song and speech the other innocently practised. The result was that the friendship of Hogg and Scott continued to the end in a very colourable imitation of brotherly love—that is to say, each had a great opinion of the other's talents coupled with an even greater opinion of his own dignity, which sometimes led to bickerings and snappings but never to downright ill-will.

The Sheriff left Ettrickhouse in a blaze of benevolence. He was now convinced that " Auld Maitland " was genuine and urged Mr. Hogg to continue his good work in view of the third volume of the *Border Minstrelsy* now in preparation. He undertook to further any other literary schemes that Mr. Hogg might have in mind, and even hoped that Mr. Hogg would soon be in the Lasswade direction. " By all means come and see me," he was kind enough to say, " and I will there introduce you to my wife. She is a foreigner as dark as a blackberry, and does not speak the broad Scots so well as you and me; of course, I don't expect you to admire her much, but I shall assure you of a welcome." Though Hogg took the welcome for granted, the information about Mrs. Scott gave him something of a shock. So the Sheriff had married one of those half-breed heiresses from the West Indies !

More than a year passed before they met again, and when they did circumstances had changed somewhat. Thanks to the good Sheriff, who had vouched for him as really and truly a genuine working shepherd of Ettrick, he had gained an entrée to the *Scots Magazine*, which had published several articles of his on a holiday trip to the Highlands. It was true the *Scots Magazine's* welcome had soon grown cold, for the series was abruptly discontinued. But that, though it annoyed the Shepherd, did not abash him in the least. His assurance, always a sturdy growth, was now immense. He was satisfied that he had graduated as a metropolitan man of letters and an original. One day towards Christmas, 1803, he presented himself at Castle Street, Edinburgh, in character, complete with blue bonnet, maud and a due amount of occupational dirt.

On being introduced to the drawing-room the Shepherd was agreeably surprised to find

that the lady of the house was not a negress after
all, but a pretty French brunette whose foreign
accent and inability to pronounce the aspirate
in her guest's name rendered her doubly enchanting. A pleasant evening was spent, and if
perhaps the host and hostess did not enjoy it as
much as the guest did, that was due to no lack
of ease and affability on his part. He helped
himself liberally to the best of Scott's liquor and
called him Wattie. He wiped his grimy shoes
on Mrs. Scott's best chintzes and called her
Charlotte. He talked incessantly, cracked hearty
hill-side jokes, told stories and even sang songs
for their entertainment, and at a late hour took
his reluctant departure as drunk as any reasonable
shepherd could wish to be. A day or two later,
on leaving Edinburgh, he wrote to express his
heartfelt thanks :

" I am afraid I was at least half-seas-over with
you, for I cannot for my life recollect what passed
when it was late. . . . If I was in the state in
which I suspect that I was I must have spoke a
very great deal of nonsense, for which I beg ten
thousand pardons. I have the consolation,
however, of remembering that Mrs. Scott kept
in company most of the time, which she certainly
could not have done had I been very rude. I
remember, too, of the filial (*sic*) injunction you
gave me at parting, cautioning me against being
ensnared by the loose women in town. I am
sure I had not reason enough left at the time to
express either the half of my gratitude for the

kind hint, or the utter abhorrence I inherit (*sic*) at those seminaries of lewdness."

II

It will be observed that Hogg's notions on the English language were as unconventional as his drawing-room manners, and he was equally well pleased with them. Some years afterwards, when he had settled in Edinburgh and was proposing to start a literary weekly to be called *The Spy*, Scott rather ill-naturedly asked him if he regarded himself as *ejusdem generis* with Addison, Steele and Johnson. "No sae yelegant, maybe, but I'll be mair oreeginal," replied the Shepherd tranquilly, and he believed it. It was easy for people like Scott and Wordsworth and John Wilson to be now facetious, now angry about the fellow's overweening vanity, but he had more reason than most people to have a good conceit of himself. Unlike Burns (whom poverty had not prevented from receiving an uncommonly good, even elaborate education), Hogg was self-taught. As a very small boy he occasionally went to the parish school of Ettrick, but the sum of his broken attendances did not amount to more than six months. Having from infancy had to earn his bread as a herd, he reached manhood practically illiterate. He could read, it is true, and always did read when a book came his way, but for many a year even reading was a sore labour to him. At twenty he had to teach himself to write, the little writing he had learned at school having long since been forgotten. It was about this time that he had the good luck to enter the service of the Blackhouse Laidlaws, who were his mother's cousins and amiable people and who, moreover, had what was rare in the Forest, a really respectable library.

During the ten happy years he spent at Black-house—perhaps the happiest years of his life—Hogg completed his education and managed to save £200. His social accomplishments were considerable. The girls liked him because he was good-looking, danced and sang well and had a coarse hearty way with him that warmed them to the very marrow. The men admired him for his skill with the fiddle, which was rough but spirited, and for his capacity for strong drink, which was impressive. All these good gifts caused him to be in great request at weddings and other convivial occasions.

Exactly when and how he commenced poet is not known. Of course there is his own story. He says that one day in the early autumn of 1796, while out with his sheep on the Braes of Yarrow, he met a daft man called John Scott, who recited the whole of " Tam o' Shanter " to him. Deeply moved, he asked the name of the author. He was told it was Robert Burns, the Dumfries gauger, lately deceased. This, he assures us, was the first he had ever heard of Burns; but finding that the position of national bard was vacant he there and then decided that James Hogg was the fittest man to fill it, and set to work at once. It would be difficult to imagine a more bare-faced lie. Burns for the last ten years of his life was a national celebrity of whom every intelligent peasant in Scotland had heard. In the first burst of his fame he had made a kind of triumphal progress through the Border counties, receiving the freedom of Dumfries, stopping with people known to Hogg, making it a particular point to visit the Vale of Ettrick. That a keen-witted young man of literary tastes who travelled freely all over the country should have been ignorant of the very existence of such a person—who, moreover, was actually living within thirty miles of him—is not to be believed for a moment.[1] Hogg himself, however, came to believe it implicitly, such is the virtue of frequent repetition.

His first literary adventure was a recruiting song, "Donald MacDonald," written during the invasion scare of 1800. It was set to music and became enormously popular, but it brought neither money nor glory. For owing to some unwonted diffidence Hogg did not choose to put his name to it, and for years never thought it worth while to claim the authorship. In 1801 he made a selection of what he deemed the best of his verses, got young Will Laidlaw to give

---

[1] If Hogg's story is true, it follows that the Laidlaws had never heard of Burns, which is absurd.

them a little polishing, and next time he was in Edinburgh with sheep gave them to a printer in the Grassmarket with an order for a thousand copies. The *Scots Magazine*, from which *Scottish Pastorals* had its one and only review, was not unkind, but advised the author "to make his rhymes answer and to attend more to grammatical accuracy." It was a poor beginning— in fact, it was no beginning at all. *Scottish Pastorals* (if he had seen it) would never have induced Scott to waste a moment's thought on Hogg. It was only the lucky chance of "Auld Maitland" a year later that brought the two men together and changed the current of the Shepherd's life.

III

HOGG's first visit to Scott in Castle Street was something more than one of courtesy. He was at a crisis—the first of many—in his affairs, wanting advice and encouragement. For the past three years he had been managing the farm of Ettrickhouse for his aged father, but the lease had lately expired and the landlord would not renew it to the Hoggs, for the simple reason that he had a prospective tenant who would pay more rent. Jamie, however, had £200 in the bank, the savings of his ten years as a hired shepherd at Blackhouse, which he considered would be enough to set him up as a sheep-farmer on his own account, and he wanted to get any advantage that the Sheriff's influence could command. Further—and this was his real motive—he wanted to have the Sheriff's opinion on some experiments in the old ballad manner that he had lately carried out. On the former matter Scott was, as usual, anxious to be helpful. As the Shepherd's fancy was towards settling in the Highlands, he gave him a sheaf of laudatory introductions to various Highland lairds. On the question of the ballads he could only express his admiration of their power qualified by some criticisms of their lack of polish. The Shepherd was well pleased. Armed with the Sheriff's introduction, he pursued his inquiries into the Highlands, and eventually found, as he thought, a suitable holding in the island of Harris, which for a Border man was so drastic and dismal a migration that he was moved to compose a "Farewell to Ettrick" on the analogy of "Farewell, Ye Bonie Banks o' Ayr" which Burns wrote when about to sail for Jamaica. What happened next is not very clear—it seems that his landlord's title was disputed in the Court of Session—but the practical result was that Jamie parted with his £200 yet did not get his farm.

It was a sad blow. The stricken Shepherd fled across the Border into Cumberland, but, finding little comfort there, came back to Scotland and hired himself to a master in Nithsdale. For the next three years he lived in the hills as a wild man, his clothes falling into rags, his only home a miserable bothy so low that he had to crawl into it on all fours. But he always had a pen and ink-horn and some sheets of paper. Gradually his spirits revived. Notwithstanding his rags and his preoccupation with sheep he somehow managed to get occasional employment as a land valuer, which brought him a few guineas in the year. He wrote more ballads, and having a good opinion of them, considered that the time was come to turn his verses into money.

He applied to Scott. Scott passed him on to Constable with a warm recommendation, and matters were quickly arranged. Constable accepted two books from the Shepherd—a volume of original ballads entitled *The Mountain Bard* and something more useful, *The Shepherd's Guide : a Practical Treatise on the Diseases of Sheep.* Both were immediately successful. By the end of 1807 Hogg found himself in possession of a literary reputation and £300 in cash. Now his postponed ambition to be a tenant farmer could be handsomely realised. Entering into partnership with an old crony called Adam Brydon, he took the farm of Locherben in Dumfriesshire. The rent he had to pay was ruinous, but he was far too happy to think of that. The future presented itself as a confused vision of sheep and dogs and dancing and fiddling and fuddling and other rustic delights, with now and then a new book of poems by the Ettrick Shepherd to be published by Constable and enthusiastically acclaimed by a discerning press and public. Such visions are not proper for men in the farming way.

Time passed. The Sheriff heard but little of the Shepherd's fortunes, and that little he did not altogether like. Becoming genuinely uneasy, he asked a mutual friend who was going into that part of the country to visit Locherben and report, providing him at the same time with a sum of money in case the Shepherd should be found in straits. This gentleman's report was, *Imprimis*, when he called, Mr. Hogg was not at home, but he was very civilly received by a person who purported to be Mr. Hogg's housekeeper, and of whom he could not help observing that she was younger and handsomer than became a bachelor establishment; *Secundo*, that when some time afterwards he paid a second visit, he found Mr. Hogg and his shearers sitting in the yard round a keg of whisky and devouring an excellent leg of mutton. The handsome housekeeper was not of the company—in fact, she was nowhere to be seen, but Mr. Hogg seemed in good spirits.

The Locherben adventure came to an untimely end soon after. The partnership with Brydon was dissolved amid recriminations. Jamie called Adam a knave and a fool, and Adam called Jamie a waster. There was much to be said on both sides. Anyhow, they went their several ways, Hogg's way being to Penpont, some miles off, where he managed to find another and humbler farm. Once the reporter already mentioned went to see how he was getting on in his new quarters. It was no beautiful housekeeper who opened the door, but "an ugly goblin of a creature," who said the master had been away for a few days but was expected home any moment. Presently Hogg turned up, showing every sign of having been on the spree for a week. He explained that he had been away looking at sheep. In fact, he had been fiddling at a neighbouring farm, where there had been a prolonged festivity. It is not surprising that the end of 1809 found him out of house and home, penniless, bankrupt and so much discredited that, for all his reputation as a shepherd, there was not a farmer in Ettrick that would hire him. He tried (droll thought!) for a commission in the militia and also (having Burns in mind) for a gauger's job, but the influential friends to whom he applied were not satisfied that his talents lay in either of these directions. The only resource left him was his pen. It had served him well before; he was resolved it should serve him better now. And so in the spring of 1810 the Ettrick Shepherd tramped to Edinburgh to set up as a professional author. He was then in his fortieth year.

The charity of two kindly tradesmen, Messrs. Grieve and Scott, who were Borderers, kept him in food and shelter while he put together a new collection of his verses, to be called *The Forest*

Minstrel (a title intended to suggest something of the same nature and quality as *The Mountain Bard*, which it was not), and approached Constable. The " Czar " received him with sour looks, but after some grumbling agreed to publish. *The Forest Minstrel* did not make a penny of profit ; but the author had had the wit to put in a dedication to the Countess of Dalkeith, who goodnaturedly took the compliment and the hint and sent him a hundred guineas. His next scheme was that experiment in " oreeginality," *The Spy*, of which mention has already been made. Scott's sneers at the project, though they might have been left unspoken, were but natural, for the Shepherd's articles in the *Scots Magazine* had not so far revealed any obvious talent for journalism. The booksellers were as sceptical as the Sheriff, and it was only after many a weary tramp through the Old Town and the New that Hogg found in Nicolson Street one Robertson, who, being habitually drunk, had a tincture of the charity that believeth all things and agreed to be responsible for *The Spy*.

The new periodical made its first appearance in September 1810, price fourpence, and, to the amazement of everybody who knew the editor, was by no means inelegant. It looked even like being a great success. But all too soon the editor's " oreeginality " became disastrously apparent. The third and fourth numbers consisted of an essay in fiction—afterwards rewritten and included in his *Tales* as *Basil Lee, or The Berwickshire Farmer*—for the incidents of which he seems to have drawn on Johnny Ballantyne's career as well as his own. It was a good story, a most moral story, suitable enough for young men but, in the opinion of many fathers of families who subscribed for *The Spy*, by no means suitable for young women. Hogg, who with his Forest upbringing belonged to the old Scotland that had no delicate airs, could not understand the importance that the town folk had begun to attach to the proper pronunciation of prunes and prisms. When they refused to continue his paper he reviled them publicly for humbugs, which only made matters worse. There was another circumstance besides the loss of half its circulation that made the conduct of *The Spy* increasingly difficult, viz. that each day on the stroke of eleven the editor was expected to accompany the publisher to a neighbouring public-house and join him in a " meridian " of whisky and rolls that lasted till late in the afternoon. After some months even the Shepherd's hardy stomach rebelled. He found another publisher.

The Spy contrived to live exactly one year, and might have lived much longer and even become a snug property if the editor had tempered his " oreeginality " with a little common sense. As it was, it was a notable *tour de force*, for, barring a few small contributions from friends, Hogg wrote every line himself. There was much in it that was clumsy and laboured, but there might have been much more; and it is possible that but for the editor's daily diet of rolls and whisky there might have been much less. Occasionally there was some excellent topical journalism. Posterity is indebted to *The Spy* for what is probably the only account of the comic side of the *Lady of the Lake* furore, which was in full blast in the year 1810–1811. Hogg was not enamoured of the poem or its *mise en scène*. He made a trip to " The Trossacks and Loch Ketturin "— his spelling of these sacred names was a deliberate defiance—and found nothing out of the ordinary to admire. An " old crusty Highlander " whom he met there was of the same opinion.

" He asked me frankly where I came from ? And what my business was in that country ? And on my informing him, that I was going to take a view of the Trossacks, he said that I was right to do so, else I would not be in the fashion, but it was a sign I was too idle, and had very little to do at home ; but that a Mr. Scott had put all the people mad by printing a lying poem about a man that never existed. What the D—— was to be seen about the Trossacks more than in a hundred other places ? A few rocks and bushes, nothing else."

The old crusty Highlander proceeded to mention certain deplorable sequelæ of the popular madness, to wit—

" that Mr. Burrel intended to build a bower in

the lonely Isle of Loch Ketturin, in which he
meant to place the prettiest girl that could be
found in Edinburgh, during the summer months,
to personate the Lady of the Lake ; that she was
to be splendidly dressed in the Highland Tartans,
and ferry the company over to the island ; that
Robert Maclean, a weaver at the Bridge of Turk,
was to be the goblin of Corrie-Uriskin, and had
already procured the skin of a monstrous shaggy
black goat, which was to form the principal part
of his dress in that capacity ; that, in fact, interest
and honour both combined to induce Maclean
to turn a goblin this very summer ; for in a conversation he had with two ladies, high in rank,
last year, he informed them, with great serious-
ness, that the goblin actually haunted the den
occasionally to this day, at stated periods, and
if they were there on such a day, at such an hour,
he would forfeit his ears if they did not see him ;
they promised him that they would come, and
reward him with a large sum of money if he ful-
filled his engagement ; that of course Robert was
holding himself in readiness to appear."

Walter Scott and the superior people of Edinburgh might laugh at *The Spy* in its lifetime and
treat its demise as an occasion for facetious commiseration, but to the poor Shepherd it was no
laughing matter. His weekly income from *The
Spy* was probably to be reckoned in shillings
rather than pounds, but while it lasted it went
some way towards providing him with all he
wanted—the humblest board and lodging and
enough whisky to make life tolerable. When
it died he had to find other means of getting the

weekly shillings. Having the national taste for controversy, he organised a kind of Cogers' Hall, called the Forum, which was open to the public at sixpence per head per meeting. Any sixpences that remained over after payment of expenses went into the pocket of the secretary, Mr. James Hogg. The meetings were held in a church in Carrubber's Close. (To English notions—and indeed to Christendom generally —the idea of club meetings in a church may seem strange and even improper; but it is to be remembered that the Scots of those days were a strict folk, very adverse to superstition, who were prepared to prove that a house made with hands could not possibly be the Lord's House except on the Lord's Day.)

The Forum did not yield much profit, but it was good publicity, and that meant a great deal to Hogg. He loved to be seen of men, but it would be a mistake to suppose that vanity was his only or even his principal motive. With the hard shrewdness of a peasant he had seen from the beginning that, for all their fair talk, the Edinburgh literary clique, of whom Scott was now the undisputed chief, had no idea of accepting him on equal terms. They would all patronise him; some, like Scott, would even be generous; but they would expect him to remember his station and deficiencies and to relapse contentedly into obscurity when the time came. Hogg remembered how Edinburgh had dealt with

Burns, and having no mind to be dished in the same way, he argued that the best means of avoiding it was to become a blatant and indefatigable self-advertiser. The procedure was simple. All he had to do was to behave the opposite of what his superior friends would have desired—that is, instead of trying to moderate his egoism and rusticity, to exaggerate them in every way. The result was the low-comedy character of " the Ettrick Shepherd," a roaring, swearing, drinking, quarrelsome, vainglorious, impudent, innocent, affectionate fantastical humorist. It was not exactly an untruthful character—he was all these things—but he had the acuteness to see that in order to play himself effectively in the limelight he needed a fairly heavy " make-up." His performance, which was carried out with wonderful verve and consistency for the rest of his life, was a great success. It involved a constant succession of unpleasant personal incidents that would have unnerved a sensitive man ; but Hogg was tough.

He was also thorough. To support the character of the Ettrick Shepherd he invented a legend of the same. He began it when he published *The Mountain Bard*, which he thought proper to preface with an autobiography in which fact and fancy were agreeably combined. Subsequently, whenever he thought that public interest in the Shepherd required stimulation, he produced new and improved versions of the autobiography which are a standing refutation of the common notion that an artist's imaginative faculties decline with advancing years. The problem of reconciling the various versions with one another and with notorious facts has provided his biographers with many a headache. We have already seen one fine specimen of his inventions—the story of how he first heard the name of Burns and resolved forthwith to be a poet. Another pleasant fiction, which he was very earnest in propagating, related to the publication of his first book. He would fain have forgotten *Scottish Pastorals*, but his enemies would not allow him. After many years they dragged the wretched thing back into the light of day and quoted elegant extracts. His answer was to invent extenuating circumstances. Once, he said, having to wait in Edinburgh between two markets and having nothing better to do, he impulsively wrote down some of his verses from memory and left them with a vile printer, who, after wickedly mutilating them, went to press without sending the author a proof! Strange to say, this story has been accepted even by Lockhart. The public were also invited to believe *inter alia* that the Ettrick Shepherd had the same birthday as Robert Burns [1]—a clear proof

[1] Hogg had a wonderful capacity for believing his own fictions. He gave the date of his birth as January 25th, 1772, and it was a great shock to the poor man when, in the last years of his life, someone pointed out that the parish register of Ettrick showed that he had been baptised on December 9th, 1770, and therefore must have been born towards the end of November—possibly on the 25th. How he came to give the wrong year as well as the wrong month is not known.

that he held the reversion of the holly-wreath by Divine appointment—and that, though born in a humble station, his blood was noble, for that unhappy surname of his, so far from having anything to do with swine or even young sheep, indicated his descent from one Haug, a viking.

After *The Forest Minstrel* three years elapsed before Hogg again approached Constable with a manuscript, but in 1813 he submitted *The Queen's Wake*, a cycle of narrative poems. Constable did not reject it, but he had doubts that prevented him from being as liberal in his terms as he usually was towards authors. In the first place it was his rule that in any bargaining about publication all the swearing and bellowing should be done by him. Hogg, who prided himself on his own talent for swearing and bellowing, could not agree to that. Secondly, having in mind the utter failure of *The Forest Minstrel*, Constable was not satisfied that Hogg had the quality that every publisher desires in an author —the power of going from strength to strength. Was he not in all probability the ordinary type of freak genius who turns out one goodish book and then writes drivel for the rest of his life? Had he not shot his bolt with *The Mountain Bard*? It was in vain that the Shepherd expatiated on the quality of *The Queen's Wake*. Constable only sniffed. The Shepherd told him that in that case he knew nothing about books, to which Constable retorted that at any rate he knew how to sell them, by God. Shaking the dust of Constable's shop from his feet, the Shepherd took his manuscript to Mr. Goldie, a promising young bookseller of large ambitions, small capital and no sense. Terms were agreed. *The Queen's Wake* was published. It was not of uniform quality, but it contained *Kilmeny*. Thenceforward there could be no question of condescension. James Hogg had taken his place among the poets.

IV

FAME is one thing, fortune quite another. The Shepherd's fame from *The Queen's Wake* was clear, but his fortune was mixed. He was able to talk as man to man—he would never talk to anybody on other terms—to Byron, Wordsworth and Southey as well as to Scott. On the other hand, there was poor young Mr. Goldie, who came under the necessity of calling a meeting of his creditors just as *The Queen's Wake* was getting well into a third edition. This apparent disaster was really Hogg's crowning mercy, for the house of Blackwood hastened to the rescue and not only salved *The Queen's Wake* but provided the author with a substantial part of his livelihood for the rest of his days. But by some mystery of accounting known only to himself Hogg made out that Goldie had diddled him of a large sum of money ; and when his next volume, *Pilgrims of the Sun,* fell flat, it seemed to him that the sooner he got returned to his sheep the better. Edinburgh bohemianism was all very well, and he enjoyed it ; but it was neither lucrative nor good for the constitution, and he was getting on in life—nearly half-way through his forties. Also he had met a young woman whom he wanted to marry. The noble lady who had helped him before, and who was now Duchess of Buccleuch, was the obvious resource. He composed a letter—probably the drollest of the begging sort ever written. After an elaborate exordium thanking her Grace for past benefactions, but assuring her that he had never really sought anything but the favour of her countenance, he proceeded :—

" I know that you will be thinking that this long prelude is to end with a request : No, madam ! I have taken the resolution of never making another request. I will, however, tell you a story which is, I believe, founded on a fact.
" There is a small farm at the head of a water called —— possessed by a mean fellow called ——. A third of it has been taken off and laid into another farm—the remainder is as yet unappropriated. Now, there is a certain poor bard, who has two old parents, each of them upwards of eighty-four years of age, and that bard has no house nor home to shelter these poor parents in, or cheer the evening of their lives. A single line from a certain very great and very beautiful lady, to a certain Mr. Riddle, would ensure that small pendicle to the bard at once. But she will grant no such thing ! I appeal to

·your grace if she is not a very bad lady that!—
I am, your grace's ever obliged and grateful,
" JAMES HOGG,
" The Ettrick Shepherd."

There is nothing like asking. The Duchess
took the unblushing request in good part. She
could not, of course, turn out the sitting tenant
just to please " a certain poor bard," but she
engaged that he should have the first vacancy.
A few months later she died, but the Duke
punctually carried out her promise. Hogg was
given the farm of Altrive Lake in Yarrow. He
took possession in 1815, sat there for the rest of
his life and was never asked for a penny of rent.[1]
The farm having been provided, there was
the stocking of it to be considered. Here, the
Shepherd argued, was an opportunity for his
eminent literary friends to emulate his Grace of
Buccleuch in being rich and plentiful in good
works. He scorned to ask them for money, but
could see no reason why he should not levy
contributions in kind. If actors had " benefit "
performances, why should not authors? His
proposal was that his friends should combine
with him to produce a " repository " of poems,
and that he should take the profits. The idea
was not received with that general enthusiasm

[1] Scottish literature owes a large debt of gratitude to the fourth
Duke of Buccleuch. It will be remembered that not long before
his generous gift to Hogg he had saved Scott from ruin by his
loan of £4,000.

that he had expected. Scott, who was the first to be approached, was positively surly in his refusal. "Ilka herring maun hing by its ain heid," he wrote, to which the infuriated Shepherd retorted with a letter which began "Damned Sir" and ended "Yours, with disgust." The intervening text was in keeping with the address and subscription, with the result that for more than a twelvemonth the Sheriff and the Shepherd were not on speaking terms.

Byron was more civil, but equally unsatisfactory. He said he hoped to do something, but didn't, which vexed Hogg so much that he wrote to John Murray about it. Murray used all his tact, pointing out that his Lordship had been much pressed with affairs of late owing to his marriage to Miss Milbanke and suggesting that the Shepherd might try the effect of a poetical appeal to Lady Byron—"a most delightful creature and possessed of an excellent temper and a most inordinate share of good sense." With simple dignity the Shepherd replied that he could do no such thing, first and foremost because "there is nothing I am so afraid of as teasing or pestering my superiors for favours"—which one takes the liberty of disbelieving—and secondly, because he had already written to Lord Byron on the occasion of his marriage wishing that Miss Milbanke "might prove both a good *mill* and a good *bank* to him, but I much doubted they would not be such as he was calculating on." The noble bridegroom's acknowledgment of the compliment had been so disagreeable as to put an end to all hopes in that quarter. "I think he felt I was using too much freedom with him," said the sagacious Shepherd.

Wordsworth was kind, but as he was the solitary volunteer his poem had to be declined with thanks. The Shepherd took a new line. If the poets would not write for him, he would write for the poets. In the space of a few weeks he composed *The Poetic Mirror*, an exercise in imitation and parody so brilliant that it would have won for Hogg a secure place in English literature even if he had never written anything else.

The Poetic Mirror was published anonymously, but the authorship was no secret. Scott was not amused, and his estrangement from Hogg might have become permanent but for the Right and Wrong Club. This curious institution lived not long, though quite long enough. It was perfectly imbecile, but is of interest as showing that once upon a time there was an Edinburgh that did not care a hang. The founder was a young barrister who had the pleasant idea of a club that as a matter of course should drink plentifully and as a point of honour should unanimously maintain any proposition whatsoever that any member might in his cups lay down. The Shepherd was a prominent member. The club met in a tavern at 5 p.m., continued its

sessions until 2 a.m. or thereabouts and then
adjourned *de nocte in noctem.* The casualty list
seems to have been heavy. It even included
Hogg, who after a severe course of meetings
drank himself into what he gently describes as
as " an inflammatory fever." The brethren
showed concern. Twice nightly—at 5 p.m.
and 2 a.m.—they sent deputations to inquire as
to his condition, which presently became so
serious that on the motion of the youngest
member, Johnny Ballantyne, the meetings were
adjourned *sine nocte* pending his recovery.
Johnny took the news to Scott, who, always
readier to forgive the Shepherd's weakness than
his strength, rushed to his aid, and had him
properly tended back to health. The breach
was healed. It was not the first nor the last, but
it was the only serious quarrel of those two great
men. Throughout their joint lives they proved
that " the falling out of faithful friend renewing
is of love."

Hogg never had any scruples about accepting
largess when it was offered or demanding it
when it was not. The logic and ethics of the
situation, as he saw it, were clear. He had merits ;
other people had money—let them give out of
their abundance. This argument, he conceived,
applied with peculiar force to Walter Scott.
Here was a man to whom fortune seemed to
have given all that is most desirable—a good
education, a modest but sufficient patrimony, a

secure and ample professional income—and now in addition his pen was earning him thousands a year, whereas the poor Shepherd, who knew he was at least the Sheriff's equal as a poet, could barely scrape a living. Hogg was not in the least envious—he had not a tinge of meanness in his nature—but he knew his own value and held that those who have all the luck of the table should be generous with their winnings. It was simply a question of the comity of authorship. With publishers he was inclined to take an even stronger line. In 1818 John Murray undertook to bring out a new edition of *The Queen's Wake*, more from a desire to do Hogg a good turn than from any hope of making money out of it. It was a troubled transaction. Hogg took the notion that Murray's heart was not in the job, scolded him for alleged delays, accused him of not advertising the book enough and wound up with a request for a loan of £50. Murray smiled and sent the money.

By this time, however, Hogg's circumstances were easier. *Blackwood's Magazine* had been started, and he was on its staff from the beginning.[1] "Maga's" earliest days were unpropitious. It had two titular joint-editors, Messrs.

[1] Some of Hogg's admirers claimed for him the honour of having founded *Blackwood*. He did not contradict them, but he never, as is sometimes said, claimed the honour himself. His own statement in the Autobiography amounts to no more than that he would have been the founder if William Blackwood had not thought of the idea first.

Pringle and Cleghorn, who would certainly have quarrelled with each other if they had not been obliged to make common cause against their employer, William Blackwood, who insisted upon keeping all the effective editorial control in his own hands. The bickering went on for six months, at the end of which Pringle and Cleghorn deserted to Constable. Blackwood was not dismayed. There were plenty of bright and briefless barristers in Edinburgh to pick and choose from. One of them was John Wilson, author of *The Isle of Palms*, who, having lately lost all his money, had now to work for his living. He was appointed " editor," and the great career of " Christopher North " began. Another of the briefless brethren, young Mr. John Gibson Lockhart, became his chief assistant. These gentlemen, having taken counsel one with another and with the Shepherd, resolved to signalise their first number in a manner suitable to their talents. They concocted a thing called " The Chaldee Manuscript," which they calculated would make Edinburgh sit up and take notice of them. They were not disappointed. Before *Blackwood* for October 1817 had been many days on sale there was such an uproar that the issue had to be called in and reprinted without " The Chaldee Manuscript." The offending item was a scurrilous attack on the late editors. Edinburgh in those days, as to-day, dearly loved gossip, and it did not mind scurrility, but at no time has the Scottish capital been able to abide a parody of the Prophet Daniel. The idea seems to have been Hogg's, but his draft was extensively "improved" by Wilson and Lockhart, who afterwards angered him very much by denying that he had any hand in it. Why three clever men should squabble over their respective shares in so dismal an exercise in facetiousness is not apparent.

With the establishment of *Blackwood* we take leave of Hogg the literary adventurer. Thenceforward he is the Ettrick Shepherd of the tales and the "Noctes Ambrosianæ." His troubles were by no means over—they never were—but he was definitely *rangé*. In 1820, in his fiftieth year, he was at last able to marry. He no longer needed to advertise himself. "Christopher North" saw to it that he should have all the publicity he wanted and a little more. The "Noctes" drew forth more than one letter beginning "Damned Sir" and ending "yours, with disgust," but complacency was always soon restored, and Wilson's rough comedy went on. The Shepherd contributed tales, articles and lyrics in amazing profusion. Nearly everything by which he is remembered belongs to his later or *Blackwood* period.

His life might have been as prosperous and serene as it was productive had he not been tempted to repeat the folly that had brought him to ruin before. Shortly after his marriage the farm of Mount Benger, which adjoined Altrive

Lake, became vacant, and Hogg must needs have it at all costs. What really attracted him to the place was that the house at Mount Benger was bigger and better than the nice little cottage he had built at Altrive Lake and afforded more facilities for entertaining—for, like his distinguished neighbour at Abbotsford, the Shepherd felt that his dignity as a public character demanded lavish hospitality—but he was easily able to convince himself that he could make it pay. There was some excuse for his optimism. He had Altrive Lake rent free; his literary work brought him a steady income, and he had expectations from his father-in-law, an Annandale farmer who passed for wealthy. But within a few months of the removal to Mount Benger the father-in-law went bankrupt and became a liability instead of an asset.

Hogg took the disaster with his usual optimism, saying how lucky it was he could offer the distressed old man the Altrive cottage for a home; but it was undeniably awkward. Counting on his father-in-law's assistance, he had been buying stock for Mount Benger pretty freely, and now he could not pay for it. Once more Sir Walter had to come to the rescue. The immediate crisis was passed, but Mount Benger never paid. There was too much hospitality both at home and at Tibbie Shiels' tavern. Somehow, though with difficulty, the Shepherd contrived to keep his literary work going. Farming was relegated to odd moments. It took five years and the imminence of bankruptcy to convince this feckless son of the soil that farming is not a spare-time job. The inevitable calamity came upon Mount Benger at the same time as it came upon Abbotsford. Scott did what he could, but naturally it was not much ; he had enough to do to keep a roof over his own head and find himself in bread and cheese. Mount Benger was abandoned. The impoverished Shepherd retired to his Sabine farm at Altrive and ended his days there. He thought—and one cannot blame him—that his work and his circumstances justified a small pension from the Royal Literary Fund, but, though Scott and Lockhart used all their influence, the Royal Literary Fund thought otherwise.

The last years of the Shepherd's life were like all the rest, consistently unlucky, yet by no means sad. In happy contrast to Scott he never knew the misery of failing mental powers. In fact, his powers seemed to grow with years and reached their acme when he was on the verge of old age. The lyrics that entitle him to his place next to Burns were written between fifty and sixty. The same year that saw Scott struck down with paralysis saw the publication of Hogg's prose masterpiece, *Memoirs and Confessions of a Justified Sinner*, a strange and terrible book which, like *Wuthering Heights*, was given to a generation incapable of appreciating it, though we cannot blame the public, seeing that the author himself never took any particular stock in it. At Christmas 1831, when Scott's lack-lustre eye was taking its first sight of the Bay of Naples, Hogg was landing at Gravesend for his first and only visit to London. He had had a rough passage from Leith and in the body was not feeling at all well, but his spirit was as strong and buoyant as ever. A new London publisher, one Cochrane, a Scotsman, had offered him specious terms for a collected edition of his tales in several volumes, and he was come to see the matter through and incidentally to accept what homage London was prepared to give him. He had no reason to complain, for London wined and dined him to his heart's content and his stomach's detriment. His expenses were confined to the price of a decent bedroom in the West End. John Murray found him in board in Albemarle Street. It was a pleasant time, but no profits accrued, for after the publication of the first volume of *Altrive Tales*, Mr. Cochrane saw fit to go bankrupt, and Hogg got nothing.

But he was incapable of profiting from experience. In little more than a year his friends learned with dismay that Cochrane, who was now in business again, had persuaded him to a new venture. Among those who had entertained Hogg in London was Mr. John James Ruskin, an Edinburgh man who managed to combine a conspicuous success in the wine and spirit trade with a fine taste in pictures and the strictest evangelical piety. It is difficult to imagine the Shepherd in Mrs. Ruskin's drawing-room, but if he committed any solecisms they seem to have been atoned for by his partiality for dear son John—then about twelve—for whom he predicted great things. At all events Mr. Ruskin liked him well enough to write him in January 1834 a very serious warning about Cochrane's financial position. " Put not your trust in booksellers," he said. " Cash is the word. But the knaves are despotic and deal in rags of bills at four months' date." However, the real purpose of Mr. Ruskin's letter was not to give advice but to get some. Did Mr. Hogg, speaking as an expert, really think that son John showed promise ?

" He is now between fourteen and fifteen and has indited thousands of lines. That I may not select I send you his last eighty or one hundred lines, produced in one hour while he waited for me in the City. Do not suppose we are fostering a poetical plant or genius or say *we keep a poet*. It is impossible for any parents to make less of a gift than we do in this, firstly from its small intrinsic value, as yet unsuspected by him ; and next because we dread the sacrifice of our off-spring to making him a victim to the pangs of despised verse, a sacrifice to a thankless world, who read, admire and trample on the greatest and the best."

The kindly Shepherd's reply was to invite

John to spend a holiday at Altrive, but that idea not appealing to the Ruskin parents, the precious child " indited " a courteous letter of refusal and thanks which fully justified his father's admiration for his facility and fecundity in words. The invitation was never renewed. Hogg's heart had already begun to give trouble, and when another year came round he was a dying man, consoled in his extremity by the reflection that with his penultimate breath he had created a bigger hubbub in Edinburgh than the most fantastic days of his strength had been able to compass. It was all over a very little book, *The Domestic Manners of Sir Walter Scott*, which he published in 1834 with the most pious intentions towards the memory of a man whom he had dearly loved. But owing to his incorrigible habit of saying simply what was passing through his mind it gave great offence. Lockhart, who was in the initial stages of the biography of the Wizard, flew into one of his cold perdurable passions. He never forgave the Ettrick Shepherd either in life or death. The Ettrick Shepherd did not greatly care—caring was never his habit. He passed away peacefully on November 21st, 1835, and, after a decent interval, his publisher, Mr. Cochrane, announced a second bankruptcy.

" I am told," wrote Hogg to Murray once, " that Gifford has a hard prejudice against me, but I cannot believe it. I do not see how any man can have a prejudice against me." In this simple and comfortable faith he lived and died. Yet no man ever excited more or harder prejudices, even among those who honestly called themselves his friends. Literary Edinburgh never ceased to regard him as an outsider, who not only refused to apologise for his graceless intrusion, but made extravagant claims for himself which he had the crowning indecency to justify by his achievements. He was perforce accepted, but he was never forgiven; and when he died there was general agreement that his good should be interred with his bones in Ettrick kirkyard and that the Ettrick Shepherd should live for posterity as a talented clown and mountebank of execrable manners and dubious literary morals. Some day justice may be done him, but at the moment his case is a sad one. Some half a dozen of his songs are remembered and sung by his fellow-countrymen under the impression that they are by Burns, and occasionally a professional critic has referred briefly to his tales in order to say that, if anything really good is to be found in them, it was probably written by somebody else.[1]

[1] E.g. Professor Saintsbury, who argues without (as he genially confesses) a scrap of evidence that *The Justified Sinner* was at least 50 per cent. the work of Lockhart.

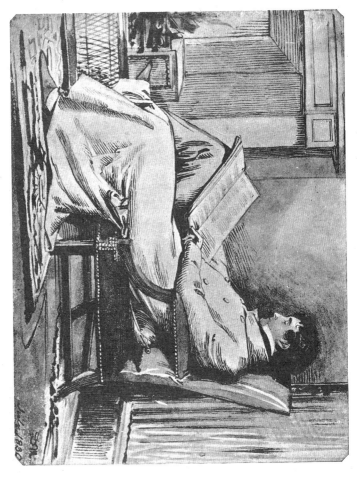

JOHN GIBSON LOCKHART

From a drawing by D. Maclise, R.A.

JOHN GIBSON LOCKHART

I

CONSIDERED simply as a human story, the life of Walter Scott is the tragedy of a great and good man who allowed his course to be guided by a vanity. Certainly in his case the ambition to found a landed family was not the paltry thing that it usually is. It was no mere projection of self-importance; it contained that baser element, but in the main it was an expression of certain political and social ideals which were as honest and generous as they were sterile and reactionary. A vanity none the less it was, a grievous fault, and grievously had Scott to answer it. But what, so to speak, happened after the fall of the curtain? What were the fortunes of the house and family that had cost so dear?

On asking these questions, we are at once confronted with the beautiful, intelligent and peculiarly ungracious visage of John Gibson Lockhart. The sequel to Scott's life is the life of his son-in-law and biographer. Like most sequels, particularly those written by another hand, it compares unfavourably with the tale it continues, but it is not uninteresting, partly by force of contrast—for, so far as was consistent with being a gentleman, a scholar and a Tory, Lockhart was everything that Scott was not— and partly because it forms the link between

Scott's day and our own. Lockhart survived his father-in-law not much more than twenty years, yet many of us who count ourselves but middle-aged find in the later annals of his life names that in our youth still stood for living men—Tennyson, Gladstone, Newman, Manning, Ruskin. When he died, at the comparatively early age of sixty, the great political controversies of his early manhood, Parliamentary Reform and Catholic Emancipation, were only memories. The Corn Laws, the old Tory Party, even the Great Duke, were dead and buried. Wordsworth, the first and last of the great Romantics, was also in his grave. The Georgian era had become historic. The tide of Victorianism had not only set in but was flowing its strongest. The cotton lords of Lancashire dictated national policy. The smoke of industry covered the land. The fine turnpike roads and swift stage-coaches, which to the opening century represented the perfect flower of progress, had been killed as dead as Queen Anne by the railroads, which now were everywhere. The new order was very grimy, very diligent, very earnest, very hopeful, very clever, but also very vague. It had a political economy but no philosophy, either of politics or of life. It was perplexed yet fascinated by the anomalous figure of Palmerston, a belated child of the eighteenth century, who could never be persuaded that in order to be serious it was necessary to be solemn.

The process of these changes was so rapid that many minds, even of the abler sort, could not adjust themselves to it. Lockhart was one of them. He was not a child of the eighteenth century; if he had been, he would have known where he stood and made the best of things. But he was born and grew up in the magnificent but uneasy years of the Romantic transition, and, having more learning and intelligence than insight, lived all his life in a state of unresolved conflict and frustration.

His parentage, while not distinguished, was, like Scott's, eminently respectable. His father, the younger son of a Lanarkshire laird, was minister of the parish of Blackfriars, Glasgow, a man of some learning, it is said, but of the strictest Whig and Presbyterian orthodoxy. His mother, Elizabeth Gibson, was a daughter of the minister of St. Cuthbert's, Edinburgh. Details of his early life are meagre. Dr. Lockhart may have been, and probably was, austere and narrow-minded, and it is possible to infer that his son found the discipline of the manse in Charlotte Street oppressive. But whatever his private reactions may have been, John Gibson Lockhart never allowed them to emerge in their nakedness. He had even more than the usual share of the middle-class Scot's abhorrence of emotional honesty when it runs counter to conventional *pietas*. Towards his father he always maintained an attitude of high esteem and even affection;

but it is significant that when he reached man's estate he repudiated the paternal politics and never lost an opportunity of expressing his hatred and contempt of Glasgow and all its ways.

His childhood was unfortunate. A severe attack of measles in infancy impaired his hearing and left him with a constitutional delicacy that he never outgrew. It says much for the quality and quickness of his intelligence that in spite of his deafness and frequent illness he was the cleverest as well as the youngest of his form at the High School of Glasgow. His lack of robustness made him physically timid. He took little or no part in the school " sports " then in vogue, which consisted chiefly in domestic fisticuffs varied by public warfare with the " keelies," [1] in which sticks and stones, as well as fists and feet, were used with much spirit and effect on both sides. Such a boy, proud in the knowledge of his intellectual superiority, can only assert himself by his wit, and wit is not the surest way to popularity. At eleven years of age,[2] when he ceased to be a schoolboy and was enrolled as a student in the College and University of Glasgow, John Gibson Lockhart was already disliked, feared and admired by a wide circle of acquaintance. His armoury consisted of brains, a power of inhibiting the display of the more

---

[1] I.e. all the town boys who did not attend the High School.

[2] A rather early but not exceptional age for matriculation at the Scottish Universities of those days. John Stuart Blackie was only eleven when he matriculated at Marischal College, Aberdeen, in 1821.

generous emotions of joy and sorrow, a reckless and malicious sense of humour, and (for a small boy) a remarkable talent for brutal caricature in the manner of Rowlandson and Gillray. At the University this character was developed and consolidated, not invariably to the youth's advantage.

In those days—and the custom was still in use within living memory—one gained a class prize, not by the professor's award, but by the vote of one's fellow-students. Merit did not as a rule suffer by that arrangement, but naturally, where merits were fairly evenly balanced, personal popularity turned the scale. In the junior Humanity class of 1806 young Lockhart, to his chagrin, found himself placed second instead of first. To console him his backers put their pence together in order to present him with a special prize on their own account—a slim octavo volume, almost overwhelmed in its ceremonial calf binding, entitled *The Lay of the Last Minstrel*, by Walter Scott, Esq. It was a welcome gift. Mr. Scott's poem had appeared in the previous year and was now in its third edition.

Lockhart spent three years at Glasgow College without any definite plans for a career. Probably, if events had followed the ordinary course, he would have drifted into the ministry, and there assuredly would have been an end of him. But in his fourth year came an incident that proved the turning-point of his life. It was the custom at Glasgow University for the best students in Latin and Greek to compete publicly for prizes " on the Blackstone." One prize in each language was awarded every year. The examination was *viva voce*. Each candidate had to undergo a rigorous catechism upon a list of books of his own choosing or—as it was technically phrased —" profession." For the purposes of the ordeal he was required to sit in a grotesque high-backed arm-chair, the seat of which was a slab of black marble—hence the term " Blackstone." Johannes Lockhart was examined on the Blackstone in 1808 for the Greek prize, and won it. The circumstances of his success were characteristic. It had come to his ears that a senior student was boasting of the portentous list of books he intended to profess. Lockhart thereupon professed the same books and beat him. The practice was sharp, but the *tour de force* admirable. It had a sequel not foreseen—Lockhart's nomination to a Snell Exhibition and his migration from Glasgow to Balliol at the tender age of fifteen years.[1]

[1] In my own time at Glasgow University the Cowan Gold Medals in Latin and Greek were awarded for " Blackstone " examinations in the manner described. Now I believe only the Latin medal is awarded on the " Blackstone," and the candidate's right to profess books has been abolished.

As to the Snell Exhibitions, their origin is curious. John Snell (born 1629) was an Ayrshire blacksmith's son, who spent a few sessions at Glasgow University but left his books to fight for King Charles in England. During the Commonwealth he was befriended by Sir Orlando Bridgeman, who made him his clerk in chambers and subsequently, on being raised to the bench, usher in his court.

II

THE young man who came down from Oxford
to live once more in a Glasgow manse was admittedly a very superior person. He had used his
four years at Oxford well. In addition to being
an excellent classic—he had taken a first in the
schools—he was widely read in English literature and had also somehow found time to acquire
a fair knowledge of French, Italian, Spanish,
Portuguese and German. To Spain and its
culture he was particularly partial, even to the
extent of having had a mild attack of Quixotism.
That is to say, he once, while at Oxford, had a
passing thought of joining Wellington in the
Peninsula—not as a combatant, of course, but
in the quality of a chaplain to the forces, for
which noble purpose he had proposed (to his
father's horror) to take Anglican orders. But
nothing had come of it, inasmuch as—owing
possibly to his enthusiasm—he had overlooked
the fact that the war would be over before he
reached the canonical age for ordination. Henceforth he was content to display his Hispanomania
by translating *romances*—he was an easy and

When Bridgeman was appointed Lord Keeper, Snell became his
seal-bearer. Later Snell entered the service of the Duke of
Monmouth as secretary and factor of his Grace's Scottish estates,
and acquired sufficient means to become lord of the manor of Uffeton
in Warwickshire. When he died in 1679 he left the residue of his
estate in trust for the education of Glasgow students at Oxford.
Beneficiaries were required to take orders in the Church of England,
but after the Revolution and the re-establishment of Presbytery
in Scotland this condition was held to be void.

elegant versifier—smoking more *cigarrillos* than were good for him and trying, not without success, to look and comport himself like an hidalgo. It was true that he had never met or even seen an hidalgo, but neither had anybody else in Glasgow, so young Lockhart's rendering passed muster. He was tall, slim, black-haired and black-browed, pale-faced, with long regular features and a small disdainful mouth. His manners were correct but not amiable. While in general an amusing he was seldom a comfortable companion, for his wit ran chiefly to mockery and even so was liable to be eclipsed by fits of most oppressive sullenness.

Oxford had done much for Lockhart—everything, in fact, but help him to the prospect of a career. There is no doubt that on pure merit he should have had a fellowship. But in those days there was a rule, unwritten but strict, that fellowships were not given to Scotsmen; and this rule (as the old-fashioned English judges used to say when defending any particularly revolting doctrine of the Common Law) was founded on reason and common sense; for it was argued that once one began that sort of thing there was no saying where it would end. That the argument was sound is obvious to anyone who considers the state of Oxford to-day, but it was hard on Lockhart. It was hard also on another Snell man, Lockhart's friend, William Hamilton. But Hamilton, with his massive

intellect and magnificent learning, was assured
of a career in any event, whereas Lockhart, who
was merely clever and accomplished, had need
of every advantage he could get. There was
another of his Oxford intimates, Jonathan
Christie, who was now reading for the English
Bar. Lockhart would have liked to do the same
—he had taken his degree in Civil Law—but the
family exchequer, which had already to support
a son in the Army, could not afford it. As for
the ministry of the Kirk, that had simply passed
into the category of the unthinkable.

For two years Lockhart idled miserably in
Glasgow. After Oxford it was very sad, though
thanks to the good libraries and dreams of escape
life might just be endured. " I think a man may
tolerate even Glasgow for half the year," he
wrote to Christie, " with the prospect of spending
the other half in company of his own choice—
and this is really an opinion of which I may speak
with some certainty, as I know not how I should
endure it at present myself, unless I had the hope
of making up for the deprivation I feel by a free
month's view of you all in summer."

There was a special cause for this qualified
complacency. As is the way of bright young
men of twenty, he was writing a novel of high
merit. It was to be called *John Todd*, and there
was to be no romantic nonsense about it—only
a mordant picture of contemporary Scottish
manners.

"My novel comes on wondrously—I mean as to bulk. My fears are many—first, of false taste creeping in from the want of any censor; secondly, of too much Scotch—from the circumstance of my writing in the midst of the 'low Lanerickshire'—&c. &c. &c. But I think I have written a great many graphical enough scenes, and have really made up my mind to print two volumes of nonsense in the spring. I think of writing to Murray, but I believe I shall put it off till I come up myself."

No doubt *John Todd* (of which we never hear again) served as a safety valve for his detestation of the low "Lanerickshire," but sometimes there were explosions. A few weeks later he was again writing to Christie :—

"I have never been so solitary in all my days as I am now and have been for some months. I feel no sympathy with the mercantile souls here, and have really no companion whatever. . . . T'other day I went to a Glasgow ball, almost, I may say, for the first time. On entering the room a buzz of 'sugars,' 'cottons,' 'coffee,' 'pullicates,' assailed my ears from the four winds of heaven. Every now and then the gemmen were deserting their partners, and rushing into the caper course to talk over samples of the morning. One sedulous dog seemed to insist on another's putting his finger into his waistcoat pocket. The being did so, and forthwith put the tip to his lips, but the countenance was so mealy that I could not tell whether it smacked of sugar or Genseng."

Hamilton was now in Edinburgh, an advocate with one client, himself, inasmuch as the first purpose to which he put his knowledge of Scots Law was to set about establishing his claim to the dormant baronetcy of Hamilton of Preston. Lockhart admired, but could not understand him. His means were small; his prospects at the Bar were negligible; yet he contemptuously refused to become a candidate for the Chair of Humanity at Glasgow, a lucrative, easy and dignified position which he might have had for the asking. Like Lockhart, though less vocal about it, he had little stomach for Glasgow. Edinburgh was not a paradise, but at least it had some people who treated life as an art and not merely a business. In the end Lockhart realised that, London and Oxford being barred, there was nothing for him but to follow Hamilton's example. The Scots Bar was just within his means. He went to Edinburgh in November 1815 and passed advocate a year later. No briefs came to him, but he was not long in finding occasional literary employment. The life was pleasant. There was Parliament Hall to be walked and talked in from ten to three or so, famous book-shops that were as good as clubs for the afternoon, and amusing taverns for the evenings when one had no invitations to dine or dance. Edinburgh was no bad place for a clever young man in those days, and wonderful value for the money. When the Long Vacation of 1817 came round Lockhart went to Germany with Hamilton—" now Sir William, at your service." He returned with the prestige of one who had been to Weimar and spoken with Goethe. The funds for the excursion had been provided by a confiding publisher, who had advanced £300 on Lockhart's undertaking to do a translation of some important German book to be determined later.[1]

The return from Germany and the events that immediately followed marked the beginning of Lockhart's career as a man of letters and settled its character. Hamilton, his senior by six years, had hitherto been the grand commander of his admiration ; but now his allegiance began to be divided between Hamilton and a still older man, who, if less gifted, was certainly more picturesque. This was a big blond beast called John Wilson, whom Lockhart had known by reputation long before he had encountered his exuberant personality in Parliament House. Wilson came from the same quarter of Scotland as Lockhart and Hamilton—he was a Paisley man—and he too had been to Oxford, but in very different circumstances from theirs. The son of a wealthy gauze manufacturer, he could boast that he was none of your beggarly Balliol Scots, but a gentleman-commoner of Magdalen with money enough to show Oxford in a manner not likely to be forgotten what real Scotsmen were made of. His

[1] The book ultimately chosen was Schlegel's *Lectures on the History of Literature.*

undergraduate exploits had passed into legend.
That he had won the Newdigate and taken an
unparalleled first in the schools was a comparatively small matter : his fame rested on the
flesh rather than the spirit. Of his prowess in
love and drink and battle all sorts of stories were
told. He had soundly thrashed the most redoubt-
able of the town bruisers. He had served as a
tavern potman in order to have access to a barmaid of whom he was enamoured. He had
joined a company of strolling players, possibly
from a similar motive. It was even said that
he had spent one vacation among the gypsies
and had espoused the gypsy king's daughter,
though some doubted.

We may discount the legends. The main
things about John Wilson are tolerably clear.
He was, in the worst sense of the term, a man's
man. We may allow that he was skilled in all
manly sports and excelled particularly in the
gentle arts of assault and battery and hard drinking ; that his wits were as powerful and versatile
as his muscles ; that his tongue was as ready and
ruthless as his fists ; that he was magnificently
generous so long as generosity was the line of
least resistance ; that he was inordinately clever,
capricious and callous, a chronic bully who had
fits of acute cowardice, and a glorious companion
who was a more than questionable friend. Having regard to these eminent qualifications, the
Town Council of Edinburgh were presently

to choose him as the fittest person to be Professor of Moral Philosophy at their University. He professed Moral Philosophy for over thirty years, and is popularly supposed to be the only really great occupant of that chair. There is a statue of him in Princes Street Gardens.

On leaving Oxford Wilson had begun life on an agreeably lavish scale. Naturally he did not go back to Paisley. Having inherited a comfortable fortune from his father and augmented it by a prudent marriage, he preferred to settle on Windermere, where he could lead the life of an affluent young country gentleman, call on Wordsworth and Coleridge when he had nothing better to do and even write a poem himself now and again. A volume of his verse entitled *The Isle of Palms*, which he published in 1812, was pronounced by the reviewers to entitle him to a place in the Lake School, which pleased but did not surprise him. Now and then he wrote an article for *The Friend*.

But this easy existence did not last long. The dishonesty of a trustee deprived Wilson of the greater part of his fortune and obliged him to do something towards earning a living. Having been called to the Scots Bar, he moved to Edinburgh, and in 1816, when Lockhart first met him, he was supposed to be holding himself out for practice. Actually briefs were the last thing he wanted. He afterwards boasted that he had never had but one and threw it up because he didn't know what the devil to do with it. He was simply waiting for something to turn up, and presently something did turn up from the same hand that fed Hogg and Lockhart—the hand of William Blackwood.

Blackwood was the rising power in Edinburgh publishing. Far inferior to Constable in genius, he was at least his equal in knowledge of the book trade and decidedly his superior in application to the detail of business. He never in his life had a really novel idea, but, being essentially a " smart " man, he was quick to follow where others had led and inventive enough to adapt their leading to his own ends. His manners were vulgar but vivacious. Everybody allowed him an abundance of energy, self-confidence and pluck ; but some added impudence. Having done well for some years as a bookseller, he had lately commenced publisher, and already dreamed of ousting Constable from his supremacy. When Johnny Ballantyne's ill-starred undertaking was wound up, Blackwood became John Murray's Edinburgh agent. In launching out, he boldly moved to the New Town, which, if Johnny Ballantyne's experience was any guide, was no place for a bookseller. But William Blackwood was a very different man from Johnny Ballantyne. His big new shop in Princes Street, with its handsome central lounge where everybody was welcome, was the wonder of

Edinburgh, and William Blackwood was always there. Business prospered.

At the moment of which we are speaking, however, Blackwood was in a fury of chagrin. A promising raid into the very heart of the Constable country had most lamentably miscarried. In the summer of 1816, after the publication of *The Antiquary*, he had been mysteriously approached by the Ballantynes with the offer to himself and Mr. Murray of a new work of fiction to be called *Tales of My Landlord*. The identity of the author was not even hinted at, but Blackwood knew at once it was Scott, and rubbed his hands gleefully at this rare stroke of luck. He had the chance of cutting out Constable for ever as far as Scott was concerned. Now, had the negotiation been in the hands of John Murray, who was all sagacity and tact and knew the man he had to deal with, it is quite possible that the connexion with Constable might have been broken, in which case Lockhart, when he came to write Scott's life, would have had a very different story to tell and a much happier one. But Blackwood was neither sagacious nor tactful—he was only fly—and his personal acquaintance with Scott was of the slightest. His flyness and ignorance were his undoing. Instead of thankfully accepting what Heaven had sent him and asking no questions, he tried to drive a sharp bargain, only to find that Scott was quite as sharp at bargains as he was and that if he did not agree quickly the *Tales* would go to Constable.

The contract proposed by Scott was peculiar in that it dealt with the publishing rights in the *first edition only*. Obviously, being, so to speak, on probation, Blackwood should have walked delicately ; but delicacy was not his way. Not content with one blunder, he must needs make a second. He criticised Scott's manuscript and suggested improvements. This was more than Scott could stand. " I have received Blackwood's impudent letter," he wrote to James Ballantyne. " Tell him and his coadjutor that I belong to the Black Hussars of literature, who neither give nor receive criticism. I'll be cursed but this is the most impudent proposal that ever was made." When *Tales of My Landlord* was published (without alteration) it ran through three editions in a few weeks. But meanwhile Blackwood had fallen out with the Ballantynes. This was the last straw. Scott had had enough of Blackwood. The fourth and subsequent editions of the book bore the imprint of Constable.

Blackwood raged furiously and threatened to have the law on everybody, but realising presently that he had not a legal leg to stand on, he subsided and began to study revenge upon Constable by other means. His plans were soon made. In the spring of 1817 he launched the *Edinburgh Monthly Magazine*.

This, as all Edinburgh knew, was an overt act of war. Hitherto Constable had had a monopoly of the Scottish periodical press, for he not only owned the great *Edinburgh Review* but also had acquired the old *Scots Magazine* and later the *Edinburgh Literary Miscellany*, which were now merged. The *Scots Magazine* was a dull, antiquated affair, and Constable meant that it should remain so: he had the sales of the *Edinburgh Review* to consider, But, as Blackwood calculated, once somebody started a vigorous new monthly, the situation would be radically altered. Constable would be in a dilemma: either he must compete on monthly lines by developing the *Scots Magazine* to the detriment of the *Edinburgh*, or look on helplessly at his quarterly's circulation being cut into by its monthly rival. At first, however, the situation did not develop according to the Blackwood plan. " The Crafty " was not the man to be hustled into precipitate action. The new venture might be a fiasco: he would wait and see. His caution was justified.

The first numbers of the *Edinburgh Monthly Magazine* were not impressive, and it soon leaked out that all was not well between Blackwood and his two joint editors, James Cleghorn and Thomas Pringle. Cleghorn was an accountant and actuary, who perhaps knew more about farm bookkeeping and life insurance than literature, but Pringle, a young Borderer who had been a clerk in the Register House, had real merits. He was an intimate friend not only of Hogg (whom he had helped with *The Poetic Mirror*), but of Will Laidlaw, whom he promptly added to the staff of the magazine, hoping thereby to bring in Scott as an occasional, perhaps a regular, contributor. He was so far successful that, while Scott could never be induced to write for the magazine, he more than once supplied it with very valuable material. Cleghorn and Pringle had no sooner been installed than they found that their position was purely nominal. On the proper conduct of the *Edinburgh Monthly Magazine* —" ma maagaz'n," as he called it—their employer had very strong views, too strong for their stomachs. After some weeks of wrangling the trouble came to a head. Cleghorn and Pringle told Blackwood he could edit his " maagaz'n " himself without their assistance, and betook themselves to Constable. The next news Edinburgh had was that, as from August, the *Scots Magazine* would appear in a new and greatly improved form under the title of *The Edinburgh Magazine and Literary Miscellany*. The new editors were Cleghorn and Pringle. Blackwood's second assault on Constable had failed even more ignominiously than the first.

Now, Blackwood had all the spirit of the gutter-snipe. He was a dirty fighter, but a game one. In his first disgust at the defection of Cleghorn and Pringle he announced that the *Monthly*

Magazine would be discontinued, and then as suddenly changed his mind. The *Monthly Magazine* would go on, but henceforth it would be called *Blackwood's Monthly Magazine*, which would be a clear intimation to all and sundry that " ma maagaz'n " was " ma maagaz'n " and nobody else's. He would be his own editor, assisted by first-class bravos who had no objection to the highest of High Tory politics and who were sensible, as he was, of the growing taste of an enlightened public for defamatory libels.[1] His choice for this noble enterprise fell upon John Wilson and John Gibson Lockhart, Jamie Hogg, who had already done good service under the Cleghorn-Pringle regime, being kept in hand as an auxiliary skirmisher. The first act of these three irresponsibles, as we have seen, was to concoct " The Chaldee Manuscript." [2]

In that notorious document Lockhart gave himself the name of " The Scorpion," and in succeeding numbers of *Blackwood* lost no time in earning it. He had the conceit, common among very young, clever and ingenuous men, that he had a fine gift of invective and that it was a thing to be proud of ; but hitherto he had not made up his mind against what or whom the precious weapon should be directed. It was at the service of anybody who would pay for it. Blackwood

---

[1] " There was a natural demand for libel at this period. The human mind had made a great advance."—Lord Cockburn's *Memorials*.

[2] *Vide* " The Ettrick Shepherd," *supra*.

engaged it for the Tories, and Lockhart was content. If a choice had to be made, he preferred the Tories : the Whigs reminded him too much of Glasgow. Henceforward anything that savoured, however faintly, of Whiggery was faithfully dealt with, to the great delight of a large and ever-growing public. Here is the sort of thing they found amusing :—

" Our hatred and contempt of Leigh Hunt as a writer is not so much owing to his shameless irreverence to his aged and afflicted king—to his profligate attacks on the character of the king's sons—to his low-born insolence to the aristocracy with whom he would in vain claim the alliance of one illustrious friendship—to his paid pandarism to the vilest passions of the mob of which he is himself a firebrand—to the leprous crust of self-conceit with which his whole moral being is indurated—to the loathsome vulgarity which constantly clings round him like a ver-mined garment from St. Giles—to that irritable temper which keeps the unhappy man, in spite even of his vanity, in a perpetual fret with him-self and all the world beside, and that shows itself equally in his deadly enmities and capricious friendships—our hatred and contempt of Leigh Hunt, we say, is not so much owing to these and other causes, as to the odious and unnatural harlotry of his polluted muse. We were the first to brand with a burning iron the false face of this kept mistress of a demoralising incendiary. We tore off her gaudy veil and transparent drapery, and exhibited the painted cheeks and writhing limbs of the prostitute."

And no doubt hilarity rose still higher when in the next number of *Blackwood* the same talented pen dealt with the folly of a poor medical student who, under the delusion that he could write poetry, had actually published an unintelligible rigmarole that began " A thing of beauty is a joy for ever" or some such nonsense. Who could have failed to admire the delicate wit with which the review ended ? " Back to the shop, Mr. John, back to plasters, pills and ointment-boxes, etc." It is said that in his later years Lockhart was prepared to admit that Keats had some merit, but the evidence is slender, and as he treated Tennyson in 1833 [1] in the same silly way as he had treated Keats in 1818, we cannot excuse him on the ground of youth and inexperience.

Of course sometimes *Blackwood* overdid it. Wilson and Lockhart were like Burke and Hare. So long as they confined their attentions to poor folk who had no friends in Edinburgh nobody minded much; but when, in the ὕβρις of long impunity, they began to pick local victims, there was trouble. One of the most respected citizens of Edinburgh was old John Playfair, Professor of Natural Philosophy at the University, who was as much beloved for his amiable personality as admired for his eminence in the science of the day. As a mathematician he ranked as the successor of the celebrated Simson of Glasgow,

---

[1] Lockhart's review in the *Quarterly* of the poems of 1833 kept Tennyson from publishing anything more for ten years.

and he is still honoured as a pioneer in the field of geology. But he happened to be a clergyman as well as a scientist—as a young man he had for some years ministered to a country parish— and also a contributor to the *Edinburgh Review* and Constable's other pet property, the *Encyclopædia Britannica*. This collocation of parts—

πρόσθε λέων, ὄπιθεν δὲ δράκων, μέσσῃ δε χίμαιρα

inspired Lockhart with the happy idea of denouncing the harmless old gentleman in *Blackwood* as an atheist, a pervert priest, "the d'Alembert of the Northern Encyclopædia." He calculated that his article would give Edinburgh a great shock, and so it did, though the shock was not of the kind expected. There were limits even to the political rancours of the capital. It was well enough to vilipend a Cockney apothecary, but an Edinburgh professor and minister of the Gospel was another matter. The Whigs were furious. The Tories were abashed. Lockhart got nothing for his pains but a few guineas from Blackwood, sour looks from everybody and some pointed reminders that people who write blasphemous parodies of Holy Writ should beware of accusing others of impiety.

A year later, when he published his first book, *Peter's Letters to his Kinsfolk*, he found it expedient to include an embarrassed apology for an outrage for which no excuse was possible and no

16   231

apology could atone.[1] The Playfair scandal passed, but a far more painful sequel to the *Blackwood* excesses was in store, and among those who found themselves innocently involved in it was Sir Walter Scott.

III

THE Scots Bar is a small society, but the smaller a society, the more it is inclined to a precise etiquette. If, on going to Edinburgh, Lockhart imagined he would have an early opportunity of meeting Scott he was doomed to disappointment. A great man like the Sheriff could not be spoken to without a formal introduction, and no introduction was forthcoming. Wilson, it is true, was on speaking terms with Scott but no more, for Scott had shown no sign of desiring to cultivate his acquaintance, and an introduction from him might have been a dubious recommendation.[2] Nearly three years elapsed before a lucky dinner invitation gave Lockhart what he had so long coveted. The meeting might easily have been a failure—for Lockhart's company manners were not good and he often

---

[1] Edgar Allan Poe, though he wrote at a somewhat later date, has given us the best criticism of *Blackwood* journalism. "How to write a *Blackwood* Article" and "The Literary Life of Thingum Bob, Esq.," though nowadays they seem painfully laboured jocularity, are really brilliant parodies. The mock reviews in the latter give a very fair idea of the critical methods of Wilson and Lockhart.

[2] "He seems an excellent warm-hearted and enthusiastic young man : something too much of the latter quality places him among the list of originals."—*Scott to Joanna Baillie*, Jan. 17th, 1812.

thought himself too much of a gentleman to behave like one—but Scott had a wonderful faculty for drawing out the best in everybody. He tactfully opened the conversation by asking about Weimar and Goethe. Lockhart was at ease at once, and discoursed with fluent intelligence. In particular he told how, on arriving at Weimar, he had asked if "Goethe the great poet" was in town but got nothing but blank looks until his landlady suggested that possibly he meant "the Herr Geheimrat von Goethe." This humble anecdote was probably worth more to Lockhart than all his enthusiasm, for it chimed with Scott's own humour. ‘He grinned broadly. "I hope," he said, " you will come one of these days and see me at Abbotsford, and when you reach Selkirk or Melrose be sure you ask even the landlady for nobody but ' the Sheriff.' "

The die was cast. Scott had decided that he rather liked the glum young man with the dark, beautiful face and the comic hidalgo airs—but how sad it was that one so young and talented should have to get his daily bread by writing for *Blackwood* ! Surely, thought the good Sheriff, he could be put into a more genteel way of earning a living. Hence it came that a few days after the memorable dinner-party Lockhart received a letter. It was from Messrs. James Ballantyne & Co. announcing that, owing to pressure of work, Mr. Scott found himself unable to continue the historical department of the *Edinburgh*

Annual Register and that if Mr. Lockhart could see his way to take it over, the firm and Mr. Scott would be greatly obliged. Mr. Lockhart saw his way with the utmost clearness to accepting a well-paid job ; but Scott was not a little vexed when presently he gathered that his *protégé* regarded the Register work as additional to and not in supersession of the beloved *Blackwood* connexion.

Still, he did not despair of weaning the youth from " the mother of mischief." Late in the fall of 1818 Lockhart and Wilson, returning to Edinburgh from Windermere, broke their journey to pay their first visit to Abbotsford. They found the Sheriff perambulating one of his callow plantations attended by the usual retinue of guests, among whom was a very great personage indeed, Robert Dundas, the second Viscount Melville. When the introductions were over Scott drew the new arrivals aside. " I am glad you came to-day," he whispered, " for I thought it might be of use to you both, some time or other, to be known to my old schoolfellow here, who is, and I hope will long continue to be, the great giver of good things in the Parliament House. I trust you have had enough of certain pranks with your friend Ebony, and if so, Lord Melville will have too much sense to remember them." What they thought about their host's loving anxiety for their welfare Lockhart has not recorded. We know, however, that they never had any occasion to test Lord Melville's capacity for forgetting. Within two years of that first visit to Abbotsford they had both established themselves comfortably in life otherwise than by political jobbery. On April 29th, 1820, Lockhart married Scott's elder daughter, Sophia, and two months later Wilson was elected Professor of Moral Philosophy in the University of Edinburgh.

Of the process by which Lockhart achieved his destiny little detail has been preserved, perhaps because little was worth preserving. Of course, the engagement created a great stir in Edinburgh, for who was this Lockhart that he should make such a marriage? Miss Scott herself was careful to tell her friends that, had she been so minded, she could have done much better. But, apart from the fact of its happening, it seems to have been a tame affair.

The same cannot be said of Wilson's advancement to the chair of Moral Philosophy, which was achieved only after a furious political battle. The University of Edinburgh is singular in being a burghal institution—it is traditionally known as " the town's college "—and until the middle of last century academic patronage was vested in the Town Council. As the Town Council was a great arena of party strife, a candidate's political colour counted for more than his merits. The election to the Moral Philosophy Chair in 1820 was fought on frankly party lines. The

Whigs were in a minority on the Council, but they had a powerful candidate, Lockhart's old friend Sir William Hamilton, and they were heartened by the fact that the best the Tories could do was John Wilson, who was an undoubted detrimental. Not only had he no special qualifications to be a professor of philosophy—that could easily be overlooked—but he was barely respectable, which was a grave fault, for Edinburgh had lately begun to attach the greatest importance to respectability. "The Chaldee Manuscript" had tainted him as a scoffer at religion; it had been remarked that he was oftener to be found in a public-house than in the bosom of his family—a habit which had been, but was no longer correct in the capital—and by some accounts boozing and blasphemy were not his only transgressions. There were Tory councillors who doubted if it would be wise to support such a person unless he were whitewashed to their satisfaction. The needful whitewashing was arranged by Lockhart and executed by Lockhart's newly acquired father-in-law.

Scott had his qualms about the champion, but he was all for the cause. Subject to a pious and privately expressed hope that the fellow, if successful, would " purge, forswear sack and live cleanly," he uttered lavish and mendacious testimonials to Wilson's worth and elevated character, and pulled every political string within his reach. He salved his conscience with the reflection that

the dignity of Moral Philosophy would possibly
be a steadying influence—

> "Invidus, iracundus, iners, vinosus, amator,
> nemo adeo ferus est ut non mitescere possit,
> si modo culturæ patientem commodet aurem."

When after a stiff fight Wilson carried the election
against the greatest philosophical mind in Britain,[1]
Scott felt obliged to write to Lockhart—

> "It is plain Wilson must have walked the
> course had he been cautious in selecting the
> friends of his lighter hours, and now, clothed
> with philosophical dignity, his friends will really
> expect he should be on his guard in this respect,
> and add to his talents and amiable disposition
> the proper degree of *retenue* becoming a moral
> teacher. Try to express all this to him in your
> own way. . . ."

These words, however, were but the prelude
to a sharp rebuke addressed to Lockhart himself.
With Wilson's victory, the conflict and its per-
sonalities should have ceased, but Lockhart must
needs emit from the pages of *Blackwood* an
unlovely shriek of triumph. It was a long poem
entitled "The Testimonium," in which Hamilton's
supporters, especially Mr. McCulloch, the editor
of *The Scotsman*, were referred to in terms that
were, even for Lockhart, exceptionally offensive.

---

[1] Hamilton received tardy recognition sixteen years later when a
reformed Town Council elected him to the Chair of Logic and
Metaphysic.

Scott was angry. The Professor of Moral Philosophy might behave like a cad if he liked, but the husband of Walter Scott's daughter must not.

"If McCulloch were to parade you on the score of stanza xiii," he wrote, "I do not see how you could decline his meeting, as you make the man your equal (*ad hoc* I mean), when you condescend to insult him by name. And the honour of such a rencounter would be small comfort to your friends for the danger which must attend it. I have hitherto avoided saying anything on this subject, though some little turn towards personal satire is, I think, the only drawback to your great and powerful talents, and I think I may have hinted as much to you. But I wished to see how this matter of Wilson's would turn before making a clean breast upon this subject. . . . Besides all other objections of personal enemies, personal quarrels, constant obloquy, and all uncharitableness, such an occupation will fritter away your talents, hurt your reputation both as a lawyer and a literary man, and waste your time in what at best will be but a monthly wonder. What has been done in this department will be very well as a frolic of young men, but let if suffice 'the gambol has been shown' . . . I am sure Sophia, as much as she can or ought to form any judgment respecting the line of conduct you have to pursue in your new character of a man married and settled, will be of my opinion in this matter, and that you will consider her happiness and your own, together with the respectability of both, by giving what I have said your anxious consideration."

Well might the young man perpend. Among its many mischiefs his association with Wilson and Blackwood had made an end of his once treasured friendship with Hamilton—an end so painful that he never afterwards could bear to speak of it—and now it was bringing the peace of his family life into peril. Had Scott been less easy-going where ties of affection or party were concerned he would not have had to apologise for delaying his remonstrance : he would have made the severance of the *Blackwood* connexion a condition of his acceptance of Lockhart as son-in-law. As it was, the admonition and the honest effort that Lockhart made to respect it came too late. Tragedy was already on its way.

There was a feeling, not confined to Edinburgh, that Blackwood had, in Scottish phrase, " gane his mile." His precious " Maagaz'n," of which he was eternally boasting, had won its magnificent circulation, at the expense of a heavy score of hatred. Lately he had been kept busy bluffing or buying off the consequential libel actions. (A particularly unpleasant one was now pending, for which the responsible party was neither Wilson nor Lockhart, but a more recent discovery of Blackwood's, one William Maginn, a distinguished graduate of Trinity College, Dublin, and a worthless, drunken rogue.) Now, in a day when impersonal journalism was the rule, one of the attractive novelties of *Blackwood* was that its most provocative articles appeared over signatures—pseudonyms, it is true, but sufficient to convey an illusion of personality. Pseudonymous journalism has since become a commonplace, but in one respect the *Blackwood* system was unique. The various pseudonyms were not appropriated, but were held by members of the staff jointly and severally, and were frequently exchanged. "Christopher North" might, and usually did, mean Wilson, but sometimes it meant Lockhart. Lockhart (*inter alia*) used the signature "Zeta," but had no exclusive property in it. Even "Olinthus Petre, D.D." was not necessarily Maginn. In these interchanges there may have been some small notion of cunning, but, as is the way with small notions of cunning, the event was unfortunate.

Blackwood had by this time a Whig rival published in London, which by its very style and title proclaimed its competitive purpose. It was called *Baldwin's London Magazine*. The editor was one John Scott, who, despite his surname, was no Borderer, but an Aberdonian with all the capacity of his breed. In Aberdeen he had been a schoolfellow of Byron's, with whom he remained a life-long friend, and in London he had made reputation as a publicist and married a daughter of Colnaghi, the famous art dealer. In the course of 1820 John Scott decided that *Blackwood's* antics were past a joke, and in the May number of *Baldwin's* he published a severe censure of the "Zeta" articles. It attracted little attention. Lockhart and Wilson never even saw it : they were far too busy campaigning for the Moral Philosophy professorship. But six months later the attack was renewed, and this time on a grand scale. John Scott had used the interval to collect what he imagined to be reliable inside information about *Blackwood*, which in three successive numbers of *Baldwin's* (November and December 1820 and January 1821) he worked up in a manner calculated to make John Bull's massive flesh creep. All the devilries of *Blackwood* were rehearsed in detail. The use of pseudonyms was held up as a deliberate attempt to deceive a guileless public that had no means of knowing they were pseudonyms. Lockhart was named as the archfiend and Sir Walter Scott as his chief aider and comforter in " an organised plan of fraud, calumny and cupidity." Finally, according to Mr. John Scott's information, Lockhart had had the hardihood to deny what was a notorious fact, viz. that he, under the name of " Christopher North," was the editor of *Blackwood*, which proved him to be a liar.

This was hard. Lockhart had quite enough on his own conscience without being saddled with the blame for Wilson's outrages and Blackwood's notions of editorship. Moreover, since Sir Walter's rebuke, he had honestly tried to reform. For months his contributions to *Blackwood* had consisted only of some translations of

Spanish ballads, his main energies being occupied in the composition of an unreadable work of fiction about ancient Rome. But such are the perils of bad company ; by his association with *Blackwood* he had brought opprobrium not only on himself but on the great man who had generously befriended him and taken him into his family. And overshadowing all these mortifying reflections was a practical issue, grim and immediate. Sophia, now seven months gone with child, might be a widow before she was a mother. For, having been publicly called a liar, Lockhart knew that he must take the course prescribed by the ethics of his age and class. He also knew his father-in-law's countenance and that he could expect no mild and dissuasive counsels from that quarter.

Accordingly, one morning early in January, Mr. John Scott had a visitor. It was Mr. Jonathan Christie, late of Balliol College, Oxford, and now of Lincoln's Inn, barrister-at-law, who stated that he called on behalf of his friend Mr. John Gibson Lockhart, who desired to know if Mr. Scott accepted responsibility for certain articles in *Baldwin's Magazine*. Mr. Scott, with the caution of his race, requested time to consider his position, which Mr. Christie, being of the same race, thought not unreasonable. At the end of two hours Mr. Scott replied in writing that " if Mr. Lockhart's motives in putting the inquiry should turn out to be such as gentlemen usually respect, there would be no difficulty experienced about giving it an explicit answer." This oracular response initiated a forty-days' debate which would have been ludicrous if the issue had been less tragic. Mr. Christie hastened to repudiate Mr. Scott's insinuation that Mr. Lockhart might be thinking of bringing an action for libel, at which Mr. Scott expressed pleasure but hinted that it would be time enough to talk about fighting when Mr. Lockhart saw fit to leave Edinburgh and show himself in London. Lockhart came up at once. John Scott thereupon undertook to give him " satisfaction " in the usual way, provided he could and would state that he had no editorial control over *Blackwood*. Lockhart's reply was that Scott, having made palpably false charges, was not entitled to any preliminary explanations.

The debate proceeded. The Caledonian Touchstones argued their point of honour with a stern adherence to principle that is beyond praise. The most amiable and ineffective of men, Horace Smith (of *Rejected Addresses*), was dragged in as Scott's " friend," who sought peace with such zeal that, thanks to his kindly efforts, the champions were presently ten times more incensed against each other than they were before. But principle triumphed over passion. There was no duel. After ten days of anxious hanging about town Lockhart was advised that he might safely " post " John Scott and go home thanking God he was rid of a knave. Accordingly he sent his adversary a common-form statement reciting *inter alia* that " Mr. Lockhart thought it necessary to inform Mr. Scott that he considered him as a liar and a scoundrel," and then took a copy of it to a newspaper for publication, with a note appended to the effect that the original had been sent to Mr. Scott, " with a notification that Mr. Lockhart intended leaving London within twenty-four hours after the time of his receiving it." The editor of the newspaper, being a good journalist, pointed out that the public could not possibly appreciate the merits of the affair unless Mr. Lockhart gave them the explanation that he denied to Mr. Scott. Lockhart agreed, and hurriedly inserted a prefatory sentence explaining that he " did not derive and never had derived any emolument from the management of *Blackwood.*" The amended document went to press, and Lockhart returned to Edinburgh by the night coach to be embraced by his wife and congratulated (with an admonition) by his father-in-law.

A week later ¹ Sir Walter himself had to go to London on official business. He found that

---

¹ In the *Life* Lockhart says " before the end of January," but this is wrong, as on February 4th Scott was writing to his son Walter that he expected to have to leave for London within a few days. He goes on to mention Lockhart's " foolish scrape " and safe return. Lockhart's reference to Scott's London visit is severely abstract and brief. He simply observes that " his letters while in London are chiefly to his own family and on strictly domestic topics." The reticence is natural.

Lockhart had left a pretty kettle of fish behind him. The "posting" statement had appeared in the press without any indication that the prefatory explanation was not part and parcel of it. John Scott's rage at what, very naturally, he took to be a crowning piece of *Blackwood* villainy knew no bounds, and it was not mitigated by Jonathan Christie's ingenuous suggestion that, having now had his explanation, he could go to Edinburgh and seek out Lockhart there. What with anxiety about his daughter's health and his son-in-law's honour Sir Walter was sorely worried. Presently, however, he was cheered by good news on both heads. Sophia had been safely delivered of a son on St. Valentine's Day, and the Duke of Wellington, whose solemn opinion had been sought, had pronounced Lockhart's conduct gentlemanly in every particular.

But even while he was writing a hasty note of congratulation to Lockhart, the farce of wounded honour was rushing to its unforeseen and tragic end. Poor perplexed Christie, with the best of intentions, had seen fit to publish a "further statement." It explained fully how the unhappy mistake had arisen and concluded— " If after this statement Mr. Scott can find any persons who believe that there was anything more atrocious than an oversight in the circumstances of the two statements, Mr. Scott is perfectly welcome to the whole weight of their good opinion." In these innocent words John Scott discerned a covert insult. He peremptorily demanded an explanation. Christie, imagining some trick, would give none, and at once found himself presented with a cartel.

On the same day (February 16th) the parties met with pistols. The rendezvous was a field at Chalk Farm at nine o'clock in the evening— a strange hour for marksmanship, but there was a bright moon. Christie's second was James Traill, Scott's Peter George Patmore.[1] A shivering Scotch surgeon named Pettigrew lurked in the background. Near by—perhaps a couple of hundred yards away—stood a famous Sunday resort of Cockaigne, the Chalk Farm Tavern, which was always ready to provide brandy and a shutter for any gentleman who had been unfortunate. After the first exchange of shots both combatants were seen standing unharmed. Christie, who as the challenged party fired first, had fired into the air, but owing to the uncertain light neither Scott nor his second had noticed it. The pistols were reloaded. Traill could not formally object to a second fire, but he was bound to indicate his opinion that after Christie's gesture the encounter should go no farther. " Gentlemen," he said—and his voice was clear and full of meaning—" before this proceeds, I must insist on one thing. You,

[1] Traill, who belonged to a well-known Orcadian family, had been at Oxford with Christie and Lockhart. He was the father of the late H. D. Traill. Patmore was the father of the poet.

Mr. Christie, must give yourself the usual chances, and not again fire in the air or fire away from Mr. Scott." Scott turned sharply towards his second. " Didn't Mr. Christie fire at me ? " he called. Some imp of perversity or ignorance took possession of Patmore. " You must not speak," he replied. " You have nothing for it now but firing." No more was said. Christie's pistol flashed, and John Scott sank to the ground. The wretched Pettigrew saw at a glance that the wound was desperate, mumbled something about having to fetch something, and fled, not to return. Scott was carried to the tavern, where he was made as comfortable as possible, and Christie and the seconds went into hiding.

Sir Walter was apprised at once. He hastened to Christie's place of retreat and learned the worst. John Scott was not expected to live. There was no need to write to Lockhart more than the simple facts : the moral needed no pointing. A few days later, however, the patient was not only still alive but showing fair promise of recovery. Sir Walter coupled the good news with a last warning :—

" You have now the best possible opportunity to break off with the magazine, which will otherwise remain a snare and temptation to your love of satire, and I must needs say that you will not have public feeling nor the regard of your friends with you should you speedily be the hero of such another scene. Forgive me pressing this.

Christie and I talked over the matter anxiously. It is his opinion as well as mine, and if either has weight with you, you will not dally with this mother of mischief any more. . . . Do not *promise*, but act, and act at once and with positive determination. Blackwood has plenty of people to carry on his magazine, but if it should drop I cannot think it fair to put the peace of a family and the life not only of yourself but of others in the balance with any consideration connected with it. This is the last word I will ever write to you or say to you on the subject." . . .

The next letter from London four days later was unexpectedly brief and weighty. John Scott was dead. Christie had fled to France. There were consequential things to be done— a distracted young wife to be convinced that her husband, though a murderer in the eyes of the law, was not likely to come to any harm ; and an aged clergyman to be written to and informed as gently as possible that his son was a fugitive from justice because he had killed a good man in a " sleeveless quarrel." [1] Sir Walter undertook these things for Lockhart's and decency's sake.

IV

BUT Lockhart continued to write for *Blackwood*. His contributions, it is true, were less frequent than formerly, and they were quite harmless,

[1] Christie and Traill, who fled with him, eventually returned and surrendered. They were tried at the Old Bailey for murder and acquitted.

but the connexion was obstinately maintained. Scott on his part kept his word never to refer to the subject again. His silence did not mean that he did not care. His remonstrances would probably have been renewed had not events deprived him of the moral authority to speak. For close on the heels of the Chalk Farm tragedy came the *Beacon* scandal, which out-*Blackwooded Blackwood* and had its own bloody sequel, and in respect of which Scott's own hands were far from clean.[1] He took what comfort he could from the reflection that at least he had managed to keep Lockhart out of the trouble.

Four years passed. Lockhart was happy enough at Chiefswood. Having to live under quasi-patriarchal conditions did not irk him as it would have irked some men. His only worries were the sickliness of little Johnny Hugh, his baby boy, and his own apparent failure to make headway in the literary world. He was always employed, to be sure, but nothing he did seemed to lead anywhere. As a novelist he had been a failure, having tried both ancient Rome (*Valerius*) and contemporary Scotland (*Adam Blair*) and made nothing of either. His *Spanish Ballads* and his annotated edition of *Don Quixote* had been well received, but one does not commonly make much reputation by translating and editing, however well. He was now collaborating with Scott in a great new edition of Shakespeare to

[1] See page 98 *ante*.

be published by Constable—more hack-work.
So far the only literary reputation he enjoyed
had been made by his *Blackwood* articles, and it
was a bad one. He could not say that his father-
in-law had allowed his interests to slumber. Sir
Walter's affections were ever of the active sort.
He extolled Lockhart's talents in and out of
season and measure, nosed about for jobs for
him, and if he did fail to get him a certain northern
sheriffdom, it was not for want of trying. For
the moment it looked as if in marrying Sophia
Scott Lockhart had shot his bolt, and that now
he would never be anything but Scott's son-in-
law. That has nearly been his fate, but not
quite. There was fortunately in the City of
London a very young man whose mission in
life was to make history, and whose first effort
in that direction happened to be Lockhart's
advancement in life. Lockhart had never met
him or even heard of him. When presently he
did meet him, he was not drawn to him, and on
better acquaintance he cordially detested him.

It was in the middle of September 1825—just
while Scott was still ruminating amazedly over
Constable's mighty project of the *Miscellany*—
that there arrived at Chiefswood a letter from
London. It was from William Wright, con-
veyancing counsel and one of the *Quarterly*
circle, who had recently been Scott's and Lockhart's guest in Edinburgh. Mr. Wright had to
state in strictest confidence, that John Murray,

with the support of a powerful financial group, was about to launch a new venture—nothing less than a Tory newspaper on an unprecedented scale, and would be glad if Lockhart would undertake the direction of it. Full particulars would be supplied by one of Mr. Murray's co-adventurers, Mr. D'Israeli, who was even now on his way to Scotland.

Lockhart's feelings were mixed. Murray no doubt meant well, but surely something had disarrayed his usually sober senses that he should be asking a *gentleman* to edit a newspaper, and surely Wright ought to have known better than to make himself the vehicle of such a proposal. On the other hand, it would be an occasion to have Mr. D'Israeli in one's house, whose name was honoured by all students of the curious in literature and history, though how the devil a fat, elderly, easy-going recluse of a Jew came to be in the newspaper business was more than the combined wits of Lockhart and Scott could fathom. Before the problem could be resolved an Oriental youth, slim, lustrous and ingratiating, presented himself at Chiefswood. The Scottish hidalgo stared aghast. "Mr. D'Israeli," he began. "Yes," responded the resplendent vision, "Mr. Benjamin D'Israeli," and looked appealingly for something like a welcome.

He had it. Scottish hospitality can cope with most situations. This one was handled so successfully by both Lockhart and Scott that Mr.

Ben went back to London with the notion (quite erroneous) that, if he had accomplished nothing else, he had at least made an excellent impression. But in the specific object of his mission he had failed. Lockhart and Scott had been quite clear that the editorship of a newspaper was not a fit occupation for a scholar and a gentleman. In vain the Hebrew child had protested that the position proposed for Mr. Lockhart was not that of *editor* of a *newspaper* but that of " Director-General of an immense organ " : even a Disraelian phrase had not magic to persuade these stubborn Scotsmen. If Lockhart were to be brought to London another formula would have to be found.

At the moment, as it happened, John Murray was troubled about the *Quarterly*. The previous Christmas, William Gifford, aged and dying, had given up the chair, much to the joy of old-stagers like Southey, who had been driven to the verge of mutiny by the way he hacked about their articles and who now looked forward to a golden age of do-as-you-please under his successor, young John Taylor Coleridge, a nephew of the poet.[1] The proprietor of the *Quarterly* was not so pleased. Mr. Coleridge was a rising Common Law barrister, already too busy in Westminster Hall to give much time to Albemarle Street. Sooner or later he must go, and on the advice of William Wright, Murray

[1] See page 124 *ante*.

decided for sooner. About the middle of October Southey, Croker and the rest of the old gang were flung into consternation by the news that owing to the demands of his practice Mr. Coleridge had resigned the editorship of the *Quarterly Review*, that Mr. John Gibson Lockhart had been appointed in his place and that Mr. Lockhart would also act as general literary adviser to the House of Murray and direct the policy of the projected newspaper.

It was an amazing appointment. Southey and Croker, furious at not having been consulted, saw a smart bit of dirty work by Sir Walter Scott. But Scott was as much amazed as anybody else. He could only think that that great and good man, Mr. Canning, who could be trusted to discern and reward merit, had been using his interest in Lockhart's behalf. Canning, as a matter of fact, knew nothing about it, but a number or two of the *Quarterly* under the new regime convinced him that Lockhart had been brought to London by Southey, Croker and Co. for the express purpose of annoying him. Nobody could understand why, without some ulterior motive, Murray should set such store upon Lockhart's services, and to this day nobody can understand. It is said that afterwards Murray himself had his moments of amazement.

Lockhart was to have a thousand a year for the *Quarterly*—£300 more than Jeffrey ever had for the *Edinburgh*—and there were to be additional

though undefined emoluments from the newspaper and the publishing business, which Sir
Walter, who was always optimistic in financial
calculations, computed would bring in a total
income of something like £3,000. Everything
was secured by bond sealed and delivered, which
was a great source of satisfaction to the Sheriff,
though of course he regretted the break-up
of the patriarchal establishment. Presently,
however, to add to other gathering worries came
a second visit from Mr. Benjamin D'Israeli.
This time the creature's mission was humbler
but even more objectionable. All he wanted
was that Sir Walter should satisfy Southey,
Croker and Co. that his son-in-law was not the
scoundrel they supposed him to be. Sir Walter
dismissed the Jew boy with a flea in his ear.
On second thoughts, however, he wrote the
required letters, which bore that, while in exuberant youth Mr. Lockhart might possibly have
been guilty of some " light satires," there could
be as little doubt of his essential probity as of
his eminent talents. No more objections were
heard. On December 5th Lockhart, with his
wife and infant, exchanged Chiefswood for Pall
Mall. Sir Walter missed them. However,
" agere et pati Romanum est," he wrote that
evening in his *Journal*. " Of all schools commend
me to the Stoics. We cannot, indeed, overcome
our affections, nor ought we if we could, but we
may repress them within due bounds and avoid

coaxing them to make fools of those who should be their masters." The sincerity of his profession of faith was soon to be tested.

V

AMONG the commodities that Lockhart took with him from Edinburgh was a large quantity of good advice, the gift of his father-in-law. He had been exhorted to make the most of his great opportunity, remembering always that he had not only a reputation to make but a reputation to live down. He must guard against his weakness for " satire " and light company. His new position would remove him from the bad old *Blackwood* associations, which was a great blessing, but where would be the advantage of leaving " Christopher North " only to take up with Theodore Hook ? Not that Sir Walter thought ill of poor Hook—he was the best friend that unhappy wit ever had—but the new editor of the *Quarterly* could not afford to take risks. The impression made upon Lockhart by these affectionate admonitions may have lasted throughout his journey to London. It certainly did not last longer. On taking over from Coleridge, he decided that the *Quarterly* needed livening up, so his first editorial act was to enlist Professor Wilson as a contributor. He found a job for Maginn on the *Representative*—such was the immense name chosen by D'Israeli for the

" immense organ "—and he did not eschew the society of Theodore Hook, either totally or in the least. On one point, however, he denied himself with a severity that filled him with the glow of conscious virtue. He had vowed never again in all his life to draw a caricature ; and he never did.

But, while he might have walked more circumspectly, he did keep clear of serious mischief-making. The misfortunes that began almost at once and followed him for the rest of his days were none of his own contriving : they were sheer bad luck. He had not been settled in London a fortnight when tidings came of calamity in the publishing world. Lockhart, though he had an uneasy feeling that Sir Walter was more deeply involved than he cared to admit, had no conception of the fatal extent of his engagements. It was not until a fortnight later, when he was summoned to see Constable at his hotel in the Adelphi, that he really became alarmed. He found the great publisher confined to his room with gout, writhing even more in spiritual than in bodily agony, raging and blaspheming against everybody and everything like a fat and florid Satan, and demanding that Lockhart should act as an agent of necessity for the purpose of pledging Scott's credit to the last farthing in a last effort to save Hurst & Robinson. The violence of the man was terrifying, but Lockhart managed to falter a refusal, having indeed no option. Before many more days were past the whole story of ruin was public property. Sir Walter Scott was a bankrupt. So was another person, but not one that Lockhart felt any reason to love. When the dust of the cataclysm in the markets had cleared away the gay young figure of Mr. Benjamin D'Israeli was nowhere to be seen. It was to reappear presently, of course, and gayer than ever, but not in the City. Meanwhile John Murray was left to carry on the *Representative* by whatever means he could. Lockhart's assistance was of little use. He had neither the knowledge nor the aptitude for newspaper work, but even if he had had the genius of a Delane he could not have saved it. From the beginning the *Representative* was a hopeless failure. Within a week or two Lockhart had to face the uncomfortable fact that Murray could not go on indefinitely throwing good money after bad, and that when the end came—which it did after six woebegone months—he would be deprived of at least half of the handsome income he had counted upon when he decided to come to London. Everything conspired to make the task of bringing out his first number of the *Quarterly* a gloomy one. Letters from Edinburgh brought nothing but ill news. Sir Walter's affairs were even worse than the worst fears had imagined. Lady Scott's state of health, from being merely unsatisfactory, had become alarming, but nothing of that could be told to her married daughter. Sophia was imminently expecting her second baby and had quite enough to fret about with little Johnny Hugh, whose trouble was now definitely known to be spinal. On April 16th she gave birth to a feeble premature male child. Before she had fully recovered she had to be told that her mother was dead. The boy was christened Walter Scott—not a very lucky name, his widowed grandfather mused sadly, but still an honourable one. " May God give him life and health to wear it with credit to himself and those belonging to him," he noted in his *Journal*.

The year 1826 made a clean and cruel cut through Lockhart's life. It began, continued and ended in sorrow. The late autumn brought him the news that a brother in India had been drowned. The swift accumulation of grief and worry took the heart out of him. He had not even the consolation of liking his job. A very short experience of the editorship of the *Quarterly* proved to him that, while his work might be light, his position was not easy. He had none of the glorious freedom that Jeffrey had enjoyed. Murray did not share Constable's detached view of the function of a proprietor, and, while considerate and in money matters extremely liberal, he insisted upon having his say. Lockhart could hardly object to that, though he might wish it were otherwise. What did exasperate him was the constant interference of Croker, who presumed a great deal too much on his political standing and long connexion with the review. While it may be that no man is indispensable, Croker had made himself uncommonly like it, and Murray was not going to quarrel with him.

Lockhart would gladly have thrown up the *Quarterly* for a Government appointment if he could have got one. But quite early in his London career he made the mortifying discovery that he was not *persona grata* in high quarters. Scott himself solicited Canning on his behalf, but Canning made it clear that, while he entertained the highest possible opinion of Sir Walter Scott, he had not the same opinion of Sir Walter Scott's son-in-law. Canning died, but his successors were no kinder. The only recognition Lockhart ever had from his party—and he had to wait until his fiftieth year for it—was the Auditorship of the Duchy of Lancaster, a poor morsel of patronage that he hated to accept but could not afford to refuse. If anything could have added to his bitterness then it was that that " Jew scamp, Ben Disraeli," had at last managed to push into Parliament and was giving himself absurd airs. Lockhart himself had once thought of Parliament, but only once ; for on mentioning the idea to Scott he had received a snub that put it out of his head for ever. For him there was to be nothing but to stick to his last.

Domestic life brought few compensations for the disappointments of work. Indeed, the last really happy incident was the birth of a daughter, Charlotte, at the beginning of 1828, and even that was clouded by the steady decline of Johnny Hugh. There was an interval of slack water, but soon the tide of misfortune was flowing again. Sir Walter's long agony began, and before it ended Johnny Hugh was dead. Anne Scott, broken by years of strain far beyond her physical and nervous strength, survived her father but nine months. By that time Lockhart had begun his laborious task of Scott's *Life.* He was a widower before he finished it. Four years later Charles Scott ended a not too prosperous career in the Foreign Office by dying of fever at Teheran. Colonel Sir Walter Scott died at sea on his way home from India in 1847. As he left no issue the estate of Abbotsford passed to Lockhart's son Walter, but there was little cause for elation in that, for Walter Scott Lockhart-Scott was a wastrel whose follies were such that on a charitable view we may ascribe them to mental disorder. But whatever Lockhart's faults of temper may have been, he was ever an affectionate—perhaps too affectionate— father, and his gentleness towards his children is in strange contrast to the acrimony that marked most of his human contacts. Nothing in all his unhappy life is more pathetic than the patience with which he bore each successive outrage on the part of his son. A point did come at last when even Lockhart's patience failed, and relations were broken off, to be resumed, however, when the wretched boy lay broken and dying at Versailles.

The death of Walter in 1853 was the last grief that Lockhart was called upon to bear. Never robust, his health had been failing for some years, and soon after Walter's death he resigned the editorship of the *Quarterly* and went to Italy for the winter. On his return he went to Scotland to his brother's house at Milton Lockhart, Lanarkshire, and thence to Abbotsford, which was now the home of his daughter, Mrs. Hope-Scott. He died at Abbotsford on November 25th, 1854, aged sixty, and was buried in Dryburgh Abbey at the feet of Sir Walter Scott. As his bones lie at Dryburgh so does his remembrance in the mind of men. He began life believing his pen capable of great things, and so it was, but not the things he wanted to write. As essayist and critic, which was his business in life, he was barely in the second class. He dabbled in imaginative writing, but he was a very minor poet, and, as Disraeli spitefully but with truth observed, a tenth-rate novelist. It was his destiny to live in literature simply as the author of the *Life of Scott*, a task from which he had no hope of profit and little of pleasure, undertaken as a duty and accomplished in circumstances of growing affliction. Thus did fame come to him when he had long since ceased to care for it.

JOANNA BAILLIE

I

THE parish church of Hampstead was built in the year 1745, when the camp at Finchley, not much more than a mile away, was the last frail defence of the Hanoverian dynasty against Prince Charlie and his Highlanders at Derby. It is a handsome, honest, Christian-gentlemanly piece of architecture. (" Damme, sir, I'm all for religion and the Established Church, but no nonsense, sir, damme ! ") Inside there is, among many others, a simple mural tablet in memory of one Joanna Baillie. Outside in the old churchyard you will find (if you are diligent and can get on the right side of the sexton) a solid altar-tomb surrounded by iron railings. The weather-worn slab on the top bears the following inscription:—

To THE MEMORY OF MRS. DOROTHEA BAILLIE
WIDOW OF JAMES BAILLIE, D.D.
PROFESSOR OF DIVINITY IN THE
UNIVERSITY OF GLASGOW
WHO DIED IN THIS PARISH SEPTEMBER 30, 1806.
ALSO TO THE MEMORY OF
JOANNA BAILLIE
DAUGHTER OF THE ABOVE, WHO WAS BORN SEPT. 11, 1762
AND DIED FEBRUARY 23, 1851.
ALSO TO THE MEMORY OF
AGNES BAILLIE
ELDER DAUGHTER OF THE ABOVE-MENTIONED
WHO WAS BORN SEPTEMBER 24, 1760, & DIED APRIL 17,
1861.

JOANNA BAILLIE
From a picture in Hampstead Parish Church.

The slab is an abstract of a notable family history. Only one name is missing, that of Matthew Baillie, M.D., brother of Joanna and Agnes, who lies in a country churchyard in Gloucestershire and has a mural tablet in Westminster Abbey. Of him something presently, but our business is with Joanna. If you leave the church and ascend a long steep alley past what is called the " additional " churchyard—it was " additional " in 1812—you will come upon a little block of early Georgian houses placed at a fork in the road. A plaque on one of them bears that Joanna Baillie, " poet and dramatist," lived there for nearly fifty years. The house, like all of its period and class, is slim and elegant. Its rooms are rather too small to be perfectly comfortable, but their incommodity will be forgiven for the sake of their cosiness, their exquisite proportions and their panelling.

The family history that ended in the churchyard of Hampstead began more than a century before in a remote landward district of East Lothian. James Baillie was born in the parish of Crichton in or about the year 1723—that is to say, he was of the same age and from the same countryside as " Jupiter " Carlyle. Also he belonged to the same decent class of landed gentry, being apparently one of the humbler members of the family of Baillie of Jerviswood. He studied arts and theology at the University of Edinburgh on the same benches with Carlyle, and he suffered the same patriotic Presbyterian alarms when the Young Pretender came to Holyrood. Some years elapsed before he got a living, but at last in 1754, through the patronage of the Duke of Hamilton's trustees, he was presented to the parish of Shotts in Lanarkshire.[1] Shotts—now a mining village that is a byword in the west of Scotland for grime and general unpleasantness—stands on the highest point of the bleak upland that is the " great divide " of the Scottish Lowlands. On reaching the Kirk of Shotts the traveller faring westward waves a good-bye to traditional civilisation, utters a prayer and hopes there may be a Providence.

Providence did very well by the Rev. James Baillie. When he came to Shotts he was a bachelor, a condition in which he did not mean to continue, for a " placed " minister ought to be a married man. But he was not precipitate. A priest's marriage should be a circumspect affair. Knowing that all his prospects of preferment lay in the county of Lanark, he decided that where his treasure was there should his heart be, and so, after a few years' deliberation, he proposed to the daughter of a neighbouring laird, Hunter of Long Calderwood in the parish of East Kilbride. Dorothea Hunter was quite willing to be the wife of the minister of Shotts,

[1] Probably through the Earl of Haddington. The earls of Haddington are a cadet branch of the Hamiltons. The sixth earl married a Baillie of Jerviswood—hence the family name, Baillie-Hamilton.

for she was no longer young—in fact, she was getting uncomfortably near forty. They were married. Mr. Baillie had every reason to be satisfied. His wife belonged not only to a very respectable family but also to a very able one. Her two brothers—William, who was older, and John, who was younger—had gone in for medicine, and had already won fame and fortune in London as teachers and practitioners.

Two children were born at the manse of Shotts—Agnes and Matthew. A third happy event was expected when the Hamilton trustees saw fit to translate Mr. Baillie from Shotts to the much more desirable charge of Bothwell. The excitement of the move seems to have upset Mrs. Baillie, for hardly was she settled at Bothwell when she gave premature birth to twin girls, one of whom did not live. The survivor was christened Joanna.

Mr. Baillie in his quiet way continued to advance. Joanna never had but the vaguest memories of Bothwell, for when she was barely four years old her father was again translated, though not to any great distance. He was now minister of the second charge of the collegiate church of Hamilton. It was with the Hamilton district that his little family had their cherished childish associations. In due course Matthew went to Hamilton High School, where he was considered a bright pupil. He had the advantage of rigorous home tuition from his father. The girls were not so well taught—in fact, for some years they were not taught at all. They were supposed to pick up education anyhow, an art for which at first Joanna seemed to have no aptitude. She was more interested in her pony than in her books. Mr. Baillie was not greatly concerned. From the little we know of him he seems to have been a typical clerical father of the better sort of his time and country, humane but chilling, liking his children on the whole, but not disposed to pay them any more attention than was their strict due, being of the opinion that the display of natural love and affection savoured of the carnal and was therefore to be avoided, especially in the case of girls.

As time went on, however, he began to have a sneaking respect for his younger daughter. Her initial backwardness suddenly disappeared. At the age of eight she could compete with and even excel her clever brother Matthew. She also showed some signs of being a character. Pondering these things, Dr. Baillie—for he was now D.D. Universitatis Glasguensis—packed off the two girls to Glasgow to be dealt with faithfully by a single gentlewoman of Highland antecedents, who was reputed to have the art of transforming healthy little hoydens into perfect little ladies. The testimony of everybody who ever knew Joanna Baillie is that the Highland gentlewoman did her work well. Presently brother Matthew came to Glasgow too, being now thirteen years of age and therefore fit to matriculate in the faculty of Arts, pending a choice of profession. Last in the family procession to Glasgow came Dr. Baillie himself to be Professor of Divinity at the University and an immensely important personage.

His greatness did not last long, for after barely three years of it he suddenly died. If Dr. Baillie had been less prudent in his choice of a wife this would have been a calamitous blow to his family. As things fell out, however, it was the making of their fortunes. Uncle William Hunter, a cantankerous but good-hearted old bachelor, took charge of them. He had for some years been laird of Long Calderwood, but was a confirmed absentee. All his interests were in London. It was not to be expected that he should abandon his practice and his great school of anatomy and his wonderful private museum in order to lead the narrow life of a small Lanarkshire laird. So, as the house at Long Calderwood was standing empty, he installed his sister and her girls there. Matthew was left in Glasgow to finish his college course, but within a year of his father's death he was awarded a Snell Exhibition and went off to Oxford. To Uncle William this was peculiarly gratifying. Having a good opinion of Matthew's abilities, he was moved to propose a career. The plan was that Matthew, while studying the humanities in term time, should during vacations make his home in Great Windmill Street and study medicine under his uncle.

There was, it is true, something more than regard for Matthew in the old man's mind. He had quarrelled violently with his brother and rival, John Hunter. The fact was that William, the senior by ten years, was just a little too elderly-brotherly. Having started John in life, he thought he was entitled to the benefit of John's researches and to claim the credit of John's discoveries as well as his own, but John did not agree. The two great brothers parted never to meet again. Human nature being what it is, we are entitled to assume that when William Hunter decided to make Matthew Baillie his successor and heir his motives were mixed. Regard for his widowed sister was doubtless one element. Resentment against his brother was certainly another one. But, whatever the motives, the choice proved excellent. Matthew was an amiable, diligent and more than apt pupil. He was eighteen when he began his medical studies. At twenty-two he suddenly entered upon his inheritance. William Hunter died in 1783, leaving the Baillies everything.[1] *Inter alia* Matthew got the family estate of Long Calderwood.

This was an embarrassment. In the ordinary course of events Long Calderwood would have

---

[1] Except his museum, which he was to have only so long as he continued a teacher of anatomy, after which it was to go to the University of Glasgow, where it now is.

gone to John Hunter, and Matthew Baillie, like
the rest of the family, felt that Uncle William
had done very wrong in allowing a private
quarrel to affect the natural destination of the
family property. A Baillie ought not to be
laird of Long Calderwood so long as there was
a Hunter living. Matthew acted promptly.
He at once conveyed Long Calderwood to Uncle
John, and brought his mother and sisters to
keep house for him in Great Windmill Street.
So was family peace restored and established.

A peasant youth in Ayrshire of whom neither
Matthew Baillie nor anybody else had heard
at that time was soon to write :—

> " A daimen icker in a thrave
> 's a sma' request ;
> I'll get a blessing wi' the lave
> And never miss't."

There was more than a " daimen icker " in Long
Calderwood, and the ensuing blessing was
correspondingly large. The young physician
never had cause to regret his generosity. His
practice grew rapidly. To an intellectual endowment inferior only to the genius of his uncles
he added a general culture and urbanity that those
great men notoriously lacked. By the time he
was thirty he was the busiest consulting physician
in London.[1]

[1] Dr. Baillie became physician-extraordinary to George III, and
was in attendance during the King's last illness. It was he also
whom Lady Byron consulted in January 1816 on the question of
her husband's mental condition. He died in 1823.

Busy as he was, Matthew Baillie could always find time to be hospitable to the right sort of people, and in particular laid himself out to receive literary company, in entertaining whom his sisters played a modest but effective part. They were small, slight girls, not at all striking, and not noticeably pretty, but pleasant looking, with the high cheek-bones and the shrewd smiling eyes that characterise a certain type of Scotswoman. They did not speak much, but when they did everybody listened. This was not because of their wit, for they had none. It was because of their accent. Matthew had a Balliol polish of sorts, but so long as they lived—and it was a very long time—Agnes and Joanna never attempted to sophisticate their vowels or compromise with their r's. They were wise virgins. Among the literary people who came to the house were a middle-aged couple, the Rev. Richmount Barbauld and his talented wife, Ann Letitia. They had for some years carried on a very humane and also profitable private school in Norfolk, until Mr. Barbauld's poor health—he was apt to be afflicted with fits of insanity—had obliged them to discontinue it. After a year's Continental travel they were now settled in the village of Hampstead, where Mr. Barbauld ministered to a Dissenting chapel of the more liberal sort. He held Arian opinions, which, when in health and spirits, he could expound very persuasively. The Barbaulds came into the Baillie circle through Dr. Denman, the fashionable obstetrician of the day, because Matthew Baillie was courting Dr. Denman's daughter Sophia, and Sophia's little brother Tommy [1] had been at the Barbaulds' school. The Baillie women, especially Joanna, took a great liking for the Barbaulds.

Several tranquil years passed. The house in Great Windmill Street might be sombre and inconvenient, as it had been built according to the notions of Uncle William, a bachelor scientist, who thought more of his dissecting room and his museum than domestic comforts, but the family that occupied it was united and happy. In 1791, however, Dr. Matthew Baillie married Miss Denman.

On personal as well as on professional grounds no match could have been more desirable, for Mrs. Matthew by her amiability and good sense had endeared herself to her husband's family. Years afterwards her sister-in-law Joanna paid her a poetic tribute as artless and virginal as anything of little Marjorie Fleming's.

> " A judgment clear, a pensive mind,
>   With feelings tender and refined ;
>   A generous heart in kindness glowing,
>   An open hand on all bestowing,
>   A temper sweet and calm and even
>   Through petty provocations given . . .
>   Blest wight, in whom these gifts combine,
>   Our dear Sophia, sister mine."

[1] Thomas, first Lord Denman, Chief Justice of the Queen's Bench.

The only drawback to the entrance of Sophia into the family was that it meant the breaking up of the old home. Great Windmill Street was abandoned. The young couple set up house in a superior way in Grosvenor Street. Old Mrs. Baillie and her daughters decided to live in the country. Thanks to Uncle William and Matthew they had ample means. They tried several places, going as far afield as Colchester, where they spent a whole year, but ultimately gravitated towards London and settled on the southern slope of Hampstead. One of the amenities of Hampstead was Mr. Barbauld's chapel. Another was the fine view over London, which inspired Miss Joanna to write :—

" It is a goodly sight through the clear air
    From Hampstead's heathy height to see at once
    England's vast capital in fair expanse,
    Towers, belfries, lengthen'd streets and structures fair.
    St. Paul's high dome amidst the vassal bands
    Of neighbouring spires, a regal chieftain stands,
    And over fields of ridgy roofs appear,
    With distance softly tinted side by side,
    In kindred grace, like twain of sisters dear,
    The towers of Westminster, her Abbey's pride,
    While far beyond the hills of Surrey shine
    Through thin soft haze, and show their wavy line."

Not much of a " sonnet " perhaps, but, bating the circumstance that the North Downs do not shine much nor is their line noticeably wavy, a very accurate description of the prospect even to-day.

The Baillies came to Hampstead in 1798.[1]
One night in that same year Miss Mary Berry—
Countess of Orford that might have been [2]—
returning late from a fashionable party, found a
parcel awaiting her. It contained a presentation
copy of a book, fresh from the press. *Plays on
the Passions* was its title, but the author's name
was not stated, and Miss Berry searched in vain
in the wrapper and in the volume itself for some
clue to the donor. She took the mysterious
gift with her to her chamber. The title was so
piquant she meant to have just one glance while
undressing. It was far on in the morning before
she so much as touched a hairpin. She could
not lay down the book until she had read it to
the uttermost line. In a week or two *Plays on
the Passions* was the main topic of discussion in
the best literary circles. There was the unprecedented novelty of it—a volume of plays that had
never been seen on any stage. And such plays !
Not since Dryden's day—this was the more
moderate opinion ; some enthusiasts gave a
much longer date—had there been their like.
The question was, who was this prodigious
dramaturge ? The general opinion was that
some established poet, essaying a new line, had
thought it wise for the moment to remain

---

[1] The first Hampstead house of the Baillies was demolished some
years ago. It was in Willow Road, near Well Walk.

[2] The elder and favourite of Horace Walpole's two Scotch
" Straw-Berries." The old gentleman had died in the previous
year.

anonymous. But the names of the established poets were canvassed in vain. Poor Mr. Cowper was not to be thought of, and Mr. Rogers was ruled out because he had *Plays on the Passions* for review and was as much mystified and as full of admiration as anyone. As for Matt Lewis, it was true that there was some cloak and dagger business, but apart from the fact that blank verse had never been much in Matt's line, how could anyone associate his name with such elevation of sentiment and such chastity of imagination ?[1]

That the poet was of the male sex nobody doubted until one day Mrs. Piozzi threw out a facetious dissent. The heroines of *Plays on the Passions*, she remarked, were apt to be ladies of thirty years or more, and where was the man who was capable of imagining a heroine who was over twenty-five ? Speculation at once took the new direction. A strong case was made out for Mrs. Radcliffe, but presently opinion hardened in favour of Dr. John Hunter's widow, author of " My Mother bids me bind my hair." This last guess was getting " warm." Nevertheless, the mystery continued until the year 1800, when the title-page of the third edition of *Plays on the Passions* revealed the author as, not Aunt Ann,

---

[1] The article in the *Dictionary of National Biography* states—on what authority I know not—that Scott was much fancied as the author. This can hardly be. When the first volume of *Plays on the Passions* appeared, Scott was still unknown to fame. He had published nothing but his translations from the German.

but her niece Joanna Baillie. Mr. Sam Rogers was greatly astonished. He had met Miss Joanna years ago in her brother's drawing-room in Great Windmill Street, and she was the last person he would have suspected for a genius. But here he was convicted by his own judgment, fortified by the testimony of practically everybody whose opinion on a literary matter was worth anything.

There had been, as the eighteenth century drew to a close, grave doubts if the new century could even approach the literary level of its predecessor—that it should rise higher was unthinkable—but now all doubts were dispelled. Just as the eighteenth century had begun with Dryden, so the nineteenth was beginning with Joanna Baillie. There was still a future for English literature.

II

THE little Scotch spinster thus honoured took everything with becoming gravity. She was neither unduly elated when Kemble and Mrs. Siddons put on the most practicable of her plays, *De Monfort*, at Drury Lane, nor unduly depressed when a few nights later they were constrained to take it off again. She was invited out a great deal, but preferred to meet her admirers in her own home, where they could also enjoy the society of her mother—now very old and quite blind— and her dear sister. Fame made little difference to her mode of life. Her main occupations continued to be supervising the kitchen, plying her needle, reading to her mother, exchanging visits with the Barbaulds and attending Mr. Barbauld's chapel every Sunday morning. She also continued to write. The year that revealed her name to the world saw also the publication of a second volume of *Plays on the Passions*, that was nearly if not quite as much admired as the first, and two years later there was a volume of miscellaneous plays (not specifically preoccupied with passions) that provoked a fresh burst of enthusiasm. Hampstead became a place of pilgrimage.

A frequent visitor was William Sotheby, the best-known literary lounger of his day, who was always welcome because he knew everybody and had all the news. One evening early in the year 1806 Mr. Sotheby brought very great news. Many years ago, he explained, when he was a young captain of dragoons stationed at Edinburgh, he had made the acquaintance of a worthy lawyer and his family, Scott by name, and had kept up the friendship, with the happy result that he now had the privilege of being on intimate terms with the second as well as with the first poet of the day. At once the latter— Miss Joanna—bubbled over with eager questions about the author of the incomparable *Lay*, to which Mr. Sotheby replied that she might judge for herself, for Mr. Scott was even now in

London, and, if it were agreeable to her, would appreciate the honour of waiting on her at an early date.

The meeting took place under Sotheby's auspices. It fell at first rather flat. Scott arrived full of enthusiasm. He had once written a play himself, but on reading *Plays on the Passions* had pushed his " Germanised brat," as he called it, into a drawer and tried to forget it. He went out to Hampstead expecting to meet a colourful personage, and what did he see ? A demure little old maid such as he knew by the dozen in Edinburgh, who was much more nimble with her needle than her tongue. He could hardly believe it. Miss Joanna on her part was even more disappointed. This great loutish lump of lameness—an honest soul, obviously, but a romantic poet—how could such things be ? The big ugly face was a sad shock. " I was fresh from the *Lay*," she confessed many years afterwards, " and had pictured to myself an ideal elegance and refinement of feature." But like the plucky little Scotswoman she was, she quickly reformed her front. " I said to myself, if I had been in a crowd and at a loss what to do, I should have fixed upon that face among a thousand, as the sure index of benevolence and the shrewdness that would and could help me in any strait ! " The moral worth of Walter Scott being manifest, a little conversation, *more Scotico*, was sufficient to bring out the æsthetic values that at the first glance had seemed to be lacking. " We had not talked long before we saw in the expressive play of his countenance far more even of elegance and refinement than I had missed in its mere lines." The visit ended with a cordiality that had the promise of tenderness. When Scott returned to Edinburgh he added Miss Baillie to his growing list of correspondents. Her letters were in refreshing contrast to Miss Seward's outpourings.[1]

That autumn old Mrs. Baillie died, and her daughters moved up the hill to Bolton House, where they were to spend the rest of their many days. It was there that in the following year their next meeting with Scott took place, he being then in London making his final researches for the *Life of Dryden*. Thenceforward there was no doubt who was the best beloved of his many women friends. The rule of imaginative genius is that the love of women is not an indulgence but a necessity of being. Scott was an exception. There is no evidence that any woman—not even Lady Forbes—ever touched the deeper issues of his life. He was not cut out for a lover. On the other hand, he had a great capacity for being the affectionate and adored brother, and, although he did not need women much, he liked

[1] " The Swan of Lichfield " was one of the afflictions of Scott's earlier career. While she lived she pestered him with letters, and when in 1809 she died, he found she had appointed him her literary executor ! He good-naturedly undertook the office, and had her literary remains published by John Ballantyne & Co., with disastrous financial results.

them immensely. Joanna Baillie has the distinction of being the only woman to stir in him a warmer feeling than simple friendship. The "Dear Miss Baillie" of the earlier letters soon slipped into "My dear Friend," which was the most that propriety would allow. He was just a little in love with her. She too was just a little in love—at any rate until Scott appeared she never seems to have had any impulse to revisit her native land. Yet in 1808, after an absence of twenty-five years and under the bleak skies of a Scottish February, the Baillie sisters undertook a hasty tour in the Highlands, of which the end was a pleasant visit to the Scotts in Edinburgh.

With the great little lady under his roof, Scott's admiration and affection burned more ardently than ever. Here was Melpomene made flesh and dwelling among men with her headquarters in a nice little house in Hampstead. It was true that her essays in comedy were lamentable, but one could not reasonably expect comedies from Melpomene. What he could not for the life of him understand was the obtuseness of the theatrical people like Kemble and Mrs. Siddons, who whenever Joanna Baillie was mentioned showed signs of wanting to change the subject. But he had influential theatrical friends besides the Kembles. He could appeal to the great Mrs. Bentley, of Covent Garden.

" We have Miss Baillie here at present," he wrote, " the best dramatic writer whom Britain has produced since the days of Shakespeare and Massinger. I hope you have had time to look into her tragedies (the comedies you may pass over without any loss), for I am sure you will find much to delight you, and I venture to prophesy you will one day have an excellent opportunity to distinguish yourself in one of her characters."

No doubt Mrs. Bentley was glad to have Mr. Scott's letter, but the excellent opportunity of distinguishing herself never arose. However, not long after this Scott became a director of Edinburgh's one theatre and brought down Henry Siddons as lessee and manager. It is not surprising in the circumstances that the Siddons management should have opened with a new play by Joanna Baillie. *The Family Legend* was not unsuccessful because it did not belong to any " passion " series, but was pure tartan romance. It reminded ancient playgoers of the Athelstaneford minister's *Douglas*.

With the publication of a third volume of *Passions* Joanna Baillie's literary career may be said to have ended. Already her star was beginning to pale. It had looked brilliant enough while it had been solitary, but now the great romantic planets had swum into the firmament.[1] Too sensible not to appreciate the facts, she

[1] But her name was still good enough in 1817 for Longmans to pay her £1,000 for *Metrical Legends of Exalted Characters*.

withdrew from competition with a quaint but dignified curtsey—that is, in 1814 she intimated to her friends that henceforth she desired to be known as *Mrs.* Joanna Baillie. Her friends were amused by this assumption of " brevet rank," as Byron called it. Scott sent a facetious and affectionate remonstrance.

" MY DEAR MRS. BAILLIE,
". . . So you have retired from your former prefix of Miss Joanna Baillie and have adopted the mere grave appellation of *Mrs.* Well, you may call yourself what you please on the backs of letters or visiting cards, but I will warrant you you never get posterity to tack either Miss or Mrs. to the Quaker-like Joanna Baillie. We would as soon have Wm. Shakespeare, Esq." . . .

In speaking of her to third parties he had long objected to any prefix. " Who ever heard of Miss Sappho ? " he said.

Only once did Joanna ever tremble in his esteem. It was a year before his death, when he was very ill and bitterly incensed against a world that seemed bent upon the destruction of everything he held precious. He was suspicious of everybody and everything. Had not James Ballantyne betrayed him over *Count Robert of Paris* and the Reform Bill ? Was not Will Laidlaw a Whig ? Even his daughters—for Sophia had come down to Abbotsford to help her sister—seemed determined to thwart him

with their exasperating solicitudes. They, poor
things, sent for Susan Ferrier, hoping that a
stranger might manage him better. Miss
Ferrier came. By absolutely devoting herself
to keeping him amused she won his good graces.
And this was the moment chosen by Joanna Baillie
to make a last and disconcerting appearance
in print. She had for many years meditated on
the teachings of Mr. Barbauld—long since dead
and gone—concerning the exact status of Jesus
Christ in the Godhead. The more she meditated
the more she was convinced of the impregna-
bility of the Arian position and the importance
of a true understanding of it. So she wrote
an acute little tract consisting of all the Christ-
ological passages in the New Testament presentation. A copy of *The Nature and Dignity of our
Lord Jesus Christ* reached Abbotsford a day
or two before the Jedburgh election. Scott
glanced through it with rising indignation.
" What has she to do with such questions ? "
he stammered angrily, and tossed the book across
to Will Laidlaw, telling him he could have it if
he liked—it should never find a place on Walter
Scott's shelves. In the *Journal* he wrote :—

" *May* 16*th and* 17*th.*—I wrote and rode as
usual, and had the pleasure of Miss Ferrier's
company in my family hours, which was a great
satisfaction ; she has certainly less affectation
than any female I have known that has stood so
high—Joanna Baillie hardly excepted. By the

way, she [Joanna] has entered on the Socinian[1] controversy, for which I am very sorry ; she has published a number of texts on which she conceives the controversy to rest, but it escapes her that she can only quote them through a translation. I am sorry this gifted woman is hardly doing herself justice, and doing what is not required at her hands. Mr. Laidlaw of course thinks it the finest thing in the world."

Poor Joanna ! She made little credit by her tract even in the quarters that were most likely to be sympathetic. She sent a copy to Canning, who acknowledged it amiably, but said that the older he grew the less he thought such things mattered.

There are three glimpses of Joanna Baillie in her old age, when she had outlived her reputation and most of her contemporaries. Lord Jeffrey, who never once gave her a favourable review, was always on terms of sincere friendship with her, especially in the later years ; and when in London he always made a point of going out to pay his respects to " the prettiest, best-dressed, kindest, happiest, and most entire beauty of fourscore that has been since the Flood." George Ticknor found her more than charming. " She talked of Scott," he says, with a tender enthusiasm that was contagious and of Lockhart with a kindness that is uncommon when

---

[1] Evidently Scott was too angry to read the tract, which expressly condemns Socinianism as equally erroneous with orthodox Trinitarianism.

coupled with his name. . . . It is very rare that
old age, or, indeed, any age, is found so winning
and agreeable. I do not wonder that Scott in
his letters treats her with more deference and
writes to her with more care and beauty than
to any other of his correspondents, however high
or titled." Harriet Martineau is more articulate
in her admiration.

"Mrs. Barbauld's published correspondence
tells of her [Joanna Baillie] in 1800 as a 'young
lady of Hampstead whom I visited and who came
to Mr. Barbauld's meeting, all the while with as
innocent a face as if she had never written a line.'
That was two years before I was born. When
I met her about thirty years afterwards, there she
was still 'with as innocent a face as if she had
never written a line!' And this was after an
experience which would have been a bitter trial
to an author with a particle of vanity. She had
enjoyed a fame almost without parallel, and had
outlived it. She had been told every day for
years, through every possible channel, that she
was second only to Shakespeare—if second;
and then she had seen her works drop out of
notice so that, of the generation who grew up
before her eyes, not one in a thousand had read
a line of her plays. Yet her serenity was never
disturbed, nor her merry humour in the least
dimmed."[1]

As she advanced in the eighties her memory
and mind decayed, and one day in 1851 she left
life as gently as she had lived it. Agnes Baillie

[1] *Autobiography*, i. 385.

survived her sister ten years and died at the age
of 100.

Joanna took the secret of her happiness with
her. What was the secret of her extraordinary
vogue? Her plays even at the height of her
fame were never regarded as particularly actable,
and now they are not even readable ; yet, with
the solitary exception of Jeffrey, the opinion of
the greatest generation of English letters since
Elizabethans ranked her as a genius of the first
order. Byron, for example, though less exuberant than Scott, could describe her as " our
only dramatist since Otway and Southerne."
Perhaps no wholly satisfactory answer can be
given. The case may be one of those literary
oddities that simply happen. An undoubted
factor in her success was that she made her
appearance at a slack time when there was very
little competition in the poetic world, and very
moderate accomplishment, combined with a little
novelty, was quite enough to win extravagant
appreciation. Another factor may be suggested.
Joanna Baillie's vogue was never popular : it
was confined to literary people, and it is the
amiable weakness of literary people that they are
apt, if they are impressed by an author's aim, to
overpraise his actual accomplishment. Joanna
Baillie, rather before her time, had, in her old-
maidish way, the brilliant idea of writing what
in modern literary jargon is called " serious " or
" psychological " drama. She succeeded because

of the idea, and failed because the task was far beyond her. For one thing, however, she deserves a remembrance that in the general oblivion that has descended on her name has been denied her. She ranks after Burns and Hogg as third of the preservers and refurbishers of Scottish folk-song. Her contribution in this kind is small—only some half a dozen pieces, but all perfect. They include " Saw ye Johnie comin' ? " " The Weary Pund o' Tow," and " Woo'd and Married and a'."

BIBLIOGRAPHY

THE principal biographical source for Scott is, of course, Lockhart's *Life*, supplemented by the *Familiar Letters* and the *Journal*. Lockhart himself has been ill-served. His *Life and Letters*, by Andrew Lang (1897), is perhaps the silliest and slovenliest work of the kind ever perpetrated, but it is all we have, and it contains information not to be found elsewhere. Professor Wilson undertook to write a life of Hogg, but all he ever did in the matter was to take possession of Hogg's papers and lose them. The Shepherd, however, was careful to write an autobiography— or rather several autobiographies. The first is prefaced to *The Mountain Bard* (1807) and the last to *Altrive Tales* (1833). They are both entertaining, but anyone who has a reasonable regard for the truth will prefer *The Ettrick Shepherd*, by Edith Batho (1927), a book that is at once conscientious and readable. Not so much can be said for *The Life and Work of Joanna Baillie*, by Margaret S. Carhart (Yale Studies in English, vol. 64, 1923), but it is conscientious.

In addition to the foregoing the following list, though far from exhaustive, includes the main authorities :—

CHAMBERS'S *Biographical Dictionary of Eminent Scotsmen*.

CHAMBERS, ROBERT : *Life of Sir Walter Scott, with Abbotsford* Notanda, by R. Carruthers. 1874.

COCKBURN, HENRY : *Life of Lord Jeffrey*. 1852.

—— *Memorials of his Time*. 1856.

CONSTABLE, THOMAS : *Archibald Constable and his Literary Correspondents.* 1873.

CRAIG-BROWN, T. : *History of Selkirkshire and Chronicles of the Ettrick Forest.* 1886.

DOUGLAS, SIR GEORGE : *James Hogg* ("Famous Scots" Series). 1899.

GARDEN, Mrs. M. G. : *Memorials of the Ettrick Shepherd.* 1903.

GIBSON, JOHN : *Reminiscences of Sir Walter Scott.* 1871.

GILLIES, R. P. : *Recollections of Sir Walter Scott.* 1837.

GORDON, Mrs. M. : *Christopher North : A Memoir of John Wilson.* 1862.

HOGG, JAMES : *Domestic Manners and Private Life of Sir Walter Scott.* 1834. (New Edition, with memoir by the Rev. J. E. H. Thomson. 1909.)

HUGHES, Mrs. MARY ANNE : *Letters and Recollections of Sir Walter Scott.* Edited by Horace G. Hutchinson.

LOCKHART, J. G. : *Peter's Letters to his Kinsfolk.* 1819.

OLIPHANT, MRS. MARGARET : *Annals of a Publishing House—William Blackwood & Sons.* 1898.

SANDS, LORD : *Sir Walter Scott's Congé.* 1929.

SCOTT, SIR WALTER : *Introductions to Author's Revised Edition of the Waverley Novels,* etc. 1829–32.

SHARPE, CHARLES KIRKPATRICK : *Letters to and from Sir Walter Scott.* Edited by W. Allardyce. 1888.

SKENE, JAMES : *Memories of Sir Walter Scott (The Skene Papers).* Edited by Basil Thomson. 1909.

SMILES, SAMUEL : *A Publisher and his Friends—Memoir of John Murray.* Revised edition 1891.

STALKER, ARCHIBALD : *The Intimate Life of Sir Walter Scott.* 1921.

STEPHEN, SIR LESLIE : Article " Sir Walter Scott " in the *Dictionary of National Biography.*

See also *passim* the *Edinburgh,* the *Quarterly, Blackwood* and the *Walter Scott Quarterly.*

INDEX

INDEX

INDEX